ABOUT THE AUTHOR

Dr Gabriel Hemery is a writer, tree photographer and silvologist (forest scientist). The author of numerous books, Gabriel writes both fiction and non-fiction and appears regularly on TV and radio talking about trees and the environment. He co-founded Sylva Foundation, an environmental charity, and is currently its chief executive. Gabriel writes a top-ranking tree blog featuring his books and award-winning photography.

www.GabrielHemery.com

Dr Gabriel Hemery

The TREE ALMANAC

2024

A Seasonal Guide to the Woodland World

ROBINSON

ROBINSON

First published in Great Britain in 2023 by Robinson

3 5 7 9 10 8 6 4 2

Copyright © Dr Gabriel Hemery, 2023
For image credits, see page 320

A CIP catalogue record for this book
is available from the British Library.

ISBN: 978-1-47214-849-0

Designed by Clare Sivell
Typeset in Minion Pro by Clare Sivell

Printed and bound in Great Britain by Clays Ltd, Elcograf S.p.A.

Papers used by Robinson are from well-managed
forests and other responsible sources.

Robinson
An imprint of
Little, Brown Book Group
Carmelite House
50 Victoria Embankment
London EC4Y 0DZ

An Hachette UK Company
www.hachette.co.uk

www.littlebrown.co.uk

TABLE OF CONTENTS

FOREWORD

I've loved trees since I first climbed a beech in our back garden as a child. I still remember its smooth, cool branches and the way it provided comfortable perches, and shade, and a quiet haven away from activity on the ground. To me, trees have so much personality I've even used them as characters in a novel.

The climate crisis has made people start to acknowledge all the things trees do for us: sequester carbon, keep us cool, prevent erosion, provide food and shelter for animals, soften landscapes. But because they live their whole lives rooted to one spot, and grow so slowly they don't seem to change, we tend to take them for granted.

Gabriel Hemery wants us not to take trees for granted. With a seductive mix of science, history and culture, this almanac encourages us to tune in to the cycles trees go through over the course of a year. I will be consulting this book as a daily reminder to look more closely at the trees I encounter each day, to understand them more deeply and to appreciate how crucial they are in making the world a better place.

Tracy Chevalier

WELCOME

Trees transcend time with a fortitude and grace that humans can only reach in their dreams or describe in works of fiction. They are time sentinels, experiencing climate change unlike any other organism, whilst their long lives are particularly vulnerable due to their immobility. There are trees alive in Britain and Ireland today which were adolescents when human society was still in its mere infancy, when we relied heavily on wood to build, transport, cook, hunt, farm and more. Our society came from the forest, the cradle of civilisation itself, and many of us will choose to be laid to rest surrounded by wood when we are of this Earth no more.

I have written this book to celebrate the majesty and minutiae of our trees, but it is impossible to do so without also acknowledging the wider context in which we all exist together. The stark reality is the fragile state of our environment. Modelling by the world's most powerful super-computers suggests that the Earth's climate could shift to an El Niño pattern during 2024. This is likely to increase global average temperatures, resulting in the first year when we might breach 1.5°C of warming compared to pre-industrial levels (representing a totemic failure to stay within the climate change limit set out in the UN Paris Agreement).

To save ourselves, and to reverse the depleting biodiversity in Britain and Ireland, we could all try to understand better our natural world and appreciate more our connection to it. Trees offer some hope and possibility. Wildwood once covered these isles and we can look to our trees again to teach us about life in all forms, whether humans, birds, mammals, plants and invertebrates.

Given the wonder of trees, it is not surprising that I chose to dedicate my life to them, but I wouldn't want the reader to confuse my passion and admiration for sentiment. I am equally inspired by a tree's utility to humans and the myriad of wildlife which it nurtures below ground, inside its shoots and timbers, and among its spreading canopy. In writing this, the first tree almanac for Britain and Ireland, I hope to share a little of my curiosity and knowledge. I wish to reconnect the reader with nature, to inspire you to observe and watch, care and play, smell and taste, and nurture and love trees.

GABRIEL HEMERY

2023

THE YEAR 2024

A new year is always a time to reflect on the previous twelve months, and to look ahead with hope and anticipation.

We can all find solace in nature, which continues to evolve stoically, oblivious to the alarming facts and figures highlighted in the Welcome, and innocent of any of the life-altering causes. When the universal seems just too big or overwhelming, focussing on simple things or on life in miniature, and taking a little time to admire the beauty and wonder of nature, can be deeply healing. This year, find a moment to listen to the wind singing in the trees, watch a spider spin its web, or forage for a wild fruit before chewing it slowly and mindfully.

2024 is a leap year, when the adjustment of an extra, added day on 29th February is required to keep our calendars and clocks in sync with the Sun and Moon. Perhaps it's the perfect opportunity to do something extraordinary or something you've long wanted to try . . . ! It is also a year in which an elusive blue moon occurs (in August). In September, a dramatic partial lunar eclipse will be visible from anywhere in Britain and Ireland as the Moon passes through the Earth's shadow, an event which is always spellbinding.

We cannot ignore evidence of depleting biodiversity and

increasing global temperatures, and we can choose to connect and take action in 2024. You don't need to become a climate activist or an active volunteer for a conservation organisation (though either would be great!). Little steps and meaningful deeds can make a difference too. If you have a garden or can volunteer in a park, install a bug hotel, erect a bat box, sow some wildflower seeds or plant some trees. For the independently bold, become a 'sapoteur' and follow the inspiring action of French author Jean Giono's shepherd by clandestinely sowing tree seeds in waste ground and field corners.

Rise up!
Sow your future!
Grow some!
Tree lore rules! [1]

HOW TO USE THIS BOOK

A compendium of useful data and information looking to the months and year ahead is an idea familiar to many of us, after all, the first almanac (or almanack) was produced in the eleventh century. Early on, almanacs soon settled on established themes, including phases of the Moon, movement of celestial bodies and detailed information about tides. They also looked forward in a prophetic sense, by exploring natural processes, religion, horoscopes and even the occult. Almanacs became the bestsellers of their time, like cookery books and biographies of the rich and famous are now. Today, the internet puts much of this information at our fingertips, yet there is still a place in our busy lives for a beautiful book, for a text that compiles and summarises for the reader, especially when it offers a little extra by translating and illuminating information through the lens of a specific theme.

Monthly chapters include regular sections describing changes in Sun and Moon with notable celestial events. Practical notes for the garden, orchard and forest outline things to do or nurture concerning the trees under your care. A section on wildlife highlights arboreal plants, animals and fungi to spot, whether in urban or rural locations. Every month includes at least one art or craft or recipe to make. Traditions and folklore connected to trees and forests link to times long past when we were more connected to the natural world (and were also more religious and superstitious). A spotlight is shone on a single tree species which is particularly notable for the month. Finally, the Celtic tree zodiac describes the characters of the relevant trees (two straddle each month). Special features are scattered throughout, exploring a wide range of tree-related topics.

A GEOGRAPHICAL NOTE

This book focusses on Great Britain and the island of Ireland. For the avoidance of doubt, Great Britain includes England, Scotland and Wales, while the island of Ireland includes the Republic of Ireland and Northern Ireland. The term 'Ireland' in this book is synonymous with 'the island of Ireland'. The country that is the United Kingdom is Great Britain plus Northern Ireland. Occasionally the names of individual nations are used, for instance when quoting official statistics or national holidays.

A NOTE ON TIMES

Times have been calculated for the centre of Britain and Ireland (a point just south of the Isle of Man). Compared to this central point, times shift and change in scale. East–west the times shift (i.e. the same day length but occurring earlier or later), while north–south times change in scale (shrinking or expanding day length depending on season).

JANUARY

As the day lengthens, so the cold strengthens.[2]

THE MONTH AHEAD

After the excitement and merriment of the Christmas period, January can feel a little daunting at first. Many traditional sayings warned of the peril in believing that spring had arrived. Yet, it is impossible not to feel some cheer when catkins appear on some trees and snowdrops emerge from the leaf litter.

For centuries, among the most important events of January has been Wassailing on Twelfth Night. A magical recipe for the unique celebratory beverage is shared on page 26.

A spotlight is shone on hazel, a small but remarkable tree which provides countless benefits to people and wildlife. Do you know the difference between a hazelnut, filbert and cobnut? This month, have a go at making your own thumb-stick from hazel.

Woodlands and parks are not as devoid of life as you may think. Take part in a woodpecker survey or hunt for signs of the endangered hazel dormouse.

Plants are dormant and January is a good time to plant trees in most areas. It is also time to complete pruning tasks for many trees in the garden, orchard and forest, but beware it's not the right time for all species. In the countryside you may be lucky to catch hedgelayers at work, or better still you could join a course and learn this ancient craft yourself.

DATES OF NOTE

 1 New Year's Day *(bank holiday)*
 2 New Year Holiday *(bank holiday, Scotland)*
 5 Twelfth Night
 6 Epiphany
 7 Orthodox Christmas Day
14 Orthodox New Year
22 St Vincent's Day
24 Tu B'Shevat
25 St Ananias's Day
25 Burns Night *(Scotland)*

OTHER SPECIAL EVENTS

MOON WOOD FELLING: 4–11th January.

PRACTICAL NOTES

Trees are in full dormancy in terms of shoot growth but that doesn't mean that all lies still within. During mild periods, roots can begin to grow, while above ground, flower buds start to swell.

IN THE GARDEN

It is a good time to plant new trees and shrubs or to lift and move existing plants. If you benefit from naturally occurring tree seedlings, dig some up and transplant them elsewhere, or pot them up and give away to neighbours, friends or family. Not all seedlings are welcome though (e.g. sycamore often germinates prolifically) and for these you will want to pull them up before they become a nuisance. Make sure all tree leaves have been swept and raked away and added to a compost bin or heap. Traditionally vines are pruned on St Vincent's Day (22nd January).

IN THE FIELD AND ORCHARD

Traditionally, hedges are often laid in January or February. Hedgelaying is an ancient country craft where the trees and shrubs in a hedge are cut and laid horizontally. The technique involves cutting the stem near its base but not all the way through it, often using a billhook. A tongue of cambium and sapwood is retained, thin enough to allow the tree to remain alive when it is lowered to the ground where it is pleached or woven together with other laid trees and stakes. Traditionally, a laid hedge was crucial for livestock farmers before wire fences were available. Not only do they look more attractive than the cruelly flailed hedges seen across most modern farms but they offer wonderful habitat for wildlife. Distinct regional styles are recognised across Britain, especially in the Devon, Dorset, Lancashire and Westmorland, Midland Bullock, north Somerset, the south of England, Welsh Border and Yorkshire. The National Hedgelaying Society is dedicated to preserving the craft and offers training (for more information go to: www.hedgelaying. org.uk).

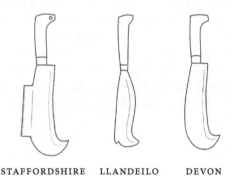

STAFFORDSHIRE   LLANDEILO   DEVON

A billhook, or simply a bill, is an agricultural tool used for cutting brash and small trees.

STAFFORDSHIRE has a double edge; a curved main blade and a straight edge along its back.

LLANDEILO has a notch to help push cut items away.

DEVON has a heavy weighted nose to help while working on hedge banks

IN THE FOREST

January is often a challenging month to plant trees because the ground is either frozen or waterlogged. In Britain, anywhere north of an imaginary line drawn between The Wash and the Severn Estuary is still a good time to plant bare-root trees, but south of this you should only plant trees grown in containers or plugs (also known as cell-grown). This simple rule is based on the fact that tree roots can start to grow in January, well before any growth in their shoots, and this can make the roots vulnerable to damage and drying out. If the soil is still intact around a tree's roots, as they are in a container, they are much better protected. In Ireland, the planting season extends until March, even for bare-root trees.

Now is a good time to prune most forest trees, whether removing branches (page 259) or formative pruning such as removing forks to improve tree shape and future quality.

If you are felling trees for timber, note that the moon wood period this month is 4–11th January (see Tree Tides on page 81).

SUN AND MOON

SUNRISE AND SUNSET

DATE	SUNRISE	SUNSET
1 JANUARY 2024, MONDAY	8:37	16:05
2 JANUARY 2024, TUESDAY	8:36	16:06
3 JANUARY 2024, WEDNESDAY	8:36	16:07
4 JANUARY 2024, THURSDAY	8:36	16:08
5 JANUARY 2024, FRIDAY	8:36	16:09
6 JANUARY 2024, SATURDAY	8:35	16:11
7 JANUARY 2024, SUNDAY	8:35	16:12
8 JANUARY 2024, MONDAY	8:34	16:13
9 JANUARY 2024, TUESDAY	8:34	16:15
10 JANUARY 2024, WEDNESDAY	8:33	16:16
11 JANUARY 2024, THURSDAY	8:32	16:18
12 JANUARY 2024, FRIDAY	8:32	16:19
13 JANUARY 2024, SATURDAY	8:31	16:21
14 JANUARY 2024, SUNDAY	8:30	16:23
15 JANUARY 2024, MONDAY	8:29	16:24
16 JANUARY 2024, TUESDAY	8:28	16:26
17 JANUARY 2024, WEDNESDAY	8:27	16:28
18 JANUARY 2024, THURSDAY	8:26	16:29

19 JANUARY 2024, FRIDAY	8:25	16:31
20 JANUARY 2024, SATURDAY	8:24	16:33
21 JANUARY 2024, SUNDAY	8:22	16:35
22 JANUARY 2024, MONDAY	8:21	16:37
23 JANUARY 2024, TUESDAY	8:20	16:38
24 JANUARY 2024, WEDNESDAY	8:18	16:40
25 JANUARY 2024, THURSDAY	8:17	16:42
26 JANUARY 2024, FRIDAY	8:16	16:44
27 JANUARY 2024, SATURDAY	8:14	16:46
28 JANUARY 2024, SUNDAY	8:13	16:48
29 JANUARY 2024, MONDAY	8:11	16:50
30 JANUARY 2024, TUESDAY	8:09	16:52
31 JANUARY 2024, WEDNESDAY	8:08	16:54

* Sunrise and sunset times have been calculated for the centre of Britain and Ireland (a point just south of the Isle of Man).

MOON PHASES

As the Earth orbits around the Sun, and the Moon orbits the Earth, the angles between the three celestial bodies change. The amount of sunlight which is reflected off the Moon that we can see from Earth changes a little every day. Gardeners have long understood that the amount of moonlight affects leaf growth, while some foresters believe it can affect wood quality (see Tree Tides, page 81). Astronomers describe eight phases of the Moon:

- new
- waxing crescent
- first quarter
- waxing gibbous

- full
- waning gibbous
- third quarter
- waning crescent

JANUARY'S MOON PHASES

4 JANUARY	◑	*Third Quarter*
11 JANUARY	●	*New Moon*
18 JANUARY	◐	*First Quarter*
25 JANUARY	○	*Full Moon*

NOTABLES

3–4TH The Quadrantids meteor shower is one of the more spectacular sights of the night sky this year, with as many as forty meteors per hour at its peak. Astronomers believe it is caused by dust grains left behind by an extinct comet. The shower appears every year between 1st–5th January and this year peaks on the night of 3rd and early morning of 4th. Meteors can appear anywhere in the night sky, with the best viewing after midnight when light from the waning gibbous moon has faded.

12TH The planet Mercury is at its highest point above the horizon in the morning sky. Look to the east just before sunrise.

25TH The first full moon of the year is commonly called the wolf moon in modern English, named after the habit of hungry wolfpacks to begin howling in the forest. The Anglo-Saxons called it 'moon after yule'.

WILDLIFE

BIRDS

Songbirds begin to sing on rare warm January days, meanwhile the rasping call of jays can be heard echoing through the leafless canopies in broadleaved woods. Take a walk through a conifer forest and pause beneath their towering and shady canopies for a chance to hear the very high-pitched 'tsp-tsp' calls of our smallest bird, the goldcrest.

Woodpeckers are among the easiest birds to identify at this time of year, even if they remain hard to spot. In broadleaved woodland, where you are most likely to find them, you have a chance of spotting them this month in the leafless tree canopies. We have three species native to Britain, though in Ireland only one species of woodpecker is present.

The great spotted woodpecker is the mid-sized species in the trio, and the one found in Ireland. About the size of a blackbird, it has distinctive black and white plumage, wears a black balaclava and has a red underside to the base of its tail. Males also have a red flash on their heads. This is a good time of year to hear them in the woods as they start 'drumming' to attract a mate, instead of singing or calling like most other

19

birds. They take a lot of care finding a patch of stem wood or a branch which is dead yet highly resonant. The 'beats' of their drumming are impossibly fast, like a masonry drill. They echo evocatively through a wood which may otherwise be quiet at this time of year.

The largest is the green woodpecker, which is almost pigeon-sized. Adults have handsome green plumage and a red cap. Despite the connotation of its name, you are more likely to see a green woodpecker on the ground near its favourite food, namely wood ants. Like all woodpeckers, it has an undulating flight. Green woodpeckers are the jokers of their kind with their 'yaffling' laugh.

The smallest of Britain's three woodpeckers is only the size of a sparrow and can be quite elusive, rarely visiting garden feeders. The lesser spotted woodpecker is black and white all over, and only the males have a red head patch. Sadly, they are now quite uncommon in Britain. They are only found in certain areas, such as the temperate rainforests of west Wales, and in very specific areas in England, such as parts of the south-west, the New Forest and Yorkshire. They are uncommon (not breeding) in Scotland. Like their next larger relative, they also drum. They have a distinctive 'kee-kee-kee' call.

Two other bird species worth looking out for in both Britain and Ireland, who share some behaviours with wood-peckers, are the colourful nuthatch and the camouflaged tree creeper.

If you are interested in woodpeckers, you can find out more and even submit sightings to the Woodpecker Network: www.woodpecker-network.org.uk.

When the woodpecker cries, rain will follow.[3]

INVERTEBRATES

Invertebrates are scarce at this time of year. Ladybirds can be spotted sheltering in the crevices of bark. Carefully turn over a log on the forest floor to reveal beetles, millipedes, centipedes, woodlice, slugs, snails and worms. On any particularly warm days this month, a bumblebee might be seen or even a butterfly such as a brimstone or green-veined white. Galls can also be easy to spot on leafless tree stems (page 155).

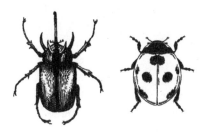

MAMMALS

January can be a good month to hunt for signs of one of our most endangered woodland mammals, the hazel dormouse. They hibernate for up to six months of the year, curled up in a tiny ball with their fury tails wrapped around them, typically among leaf litter under a tree or hedge. If you are lucky enough to find one, don't disturb it.

Hazel dormice feed almost exclusively on hazelnuts, so areas of old hazel coppice provide perfect habitat. They aren't the only small mammal to feast off hazelnuts. Fortunately, dormice adopt a very specific technique to reach the nut kernel. They nibble their way through a nut only when it is green, leaving a smooth rim with toothmarks at an angle to the hole, almost as if they have manufactured a miniature clog in the process. Voles and wood mice gnaw through the shells in a less organised fashion, leaving toothmarks across the rim of the hole. Meanwhile, squirrels and birds like the jay will simply crack the shell open. A small hand lens is a great help in spotting the tell-tale signs.

The People's Trust for Endangered Species (PTES) run a dormouse monitoring scheme and welcome volunteer spotters: ptes.org/campaigns/dormice.

PLANTS

It is a quiet month for woodland plants. Clumps of mistletoe (page 298) are easy to spot in the leafless canopies of many tree species, but especially apple, hawthorn and poplar. On the woodland floor, snowdrop and winter aconite are the first flowers of the year.

FUNGI

The depth of winter is not known for fungal forays but that doesn't mean there's nothing to spot. Bracket fungi often persist throughout the year. Look for the aptly named turkeytail or the beefsteak fungus which drips sticky red residue freakily similar to blood. The hoof fungus, which looks just like a horse's hoof, is quite common on birch trees. The easiest fungi to identify, and the most common, are King Alfred's cakes, resembling small lumps of coal (or burnt cake!). They make excellent tinder for starting fires, although the smoke is a little pungent. With grass generally not growing at this time of year, the fertilising effect of symbiotic fungi is often very prominent in the form of fairy rings around the fringes of tree roots, where the grass will be noticeably darker and longer.

TRADITION AND FOLKLORE

After the winter solstice and the end of yule, our ancestors will have waited anxiously for days to lengthen again and for the Sun to slowly begin to gain in strength. Towards the end of the month, these changes become more obvious, bringing a sense of relief, even to us in modern times.

WASSAILING

Wassailing is an ancient custom right across Europe (having been first introduced by the Vikings) and its name translates as 'be healthy'. It was a tradition celebrated after Twelfth Night (5th January) or sometimes with the upcoming full moon, when orchards were visited by carolers, particularly in cider-producing regions across Britain. People would sing and shout to encourage the sap to rise in the trees and to wake the orchard from its winter sleep, and the trees blessed to ensure a bountiful harvest. A hot mulled cider was prepared mixing a strong ale with crab apples and shared in a wassail bowl (page 26).

Various songs were traditionally sung, perhaps the best-known being, 'Here we come a-wassailing'. Here are the opening verses:

Here we come a-wassailing
among the leaves so green;
here we come a-wand'ring
so fair to be seen.

REFRAIN:
Love and joy come to you,
and to you your wassail too;
and God bless you and send you a happy new year
and God send you a happy new year.

Our wassail cup is made
of the rosemary tree,
and so is your beer
of the best barley.

REFRAIN[4]

PLOUGH MONDAY

The first Monday after Epiphany is known as Plough Monday, which this year falls on 8th January. Traditionally, farm workers would take the day off and go to church to have the plough blessed, and then drag it through the village or town with much merriment, demanding donations of cash, food or drink. If any dare refuse, the workers would attempt to plough up the victim's front garden. Normally of course, the plough will have been pulled by heavy horses or even better, by oxen. The great wooden yoke carried between these beasts of burden needed to be immensely strong. For this 'beam between horns', the best wood came from . . . the hornbeam of course.

ARTS AND CRAFTS

A RECIPE FOR OLD ENGLISH WASSAIL

A wassail is the celebratory drink prepared to toast the good health and future bounty of an orchard (page 24). It is not unlike mulled wine but uses apples, which are mixed with strong alcohol. Some recipes suggest mixing in raw whisked eggs to create a rich frothy drink, but this is optional. Crab apples were the traditional fruit used. These can often be found growing wild in hedgerows, typically fruiting prolifically, their bright yellow fruits littering the ground underneath their small canopies.

MAKES AROUND 3.5L

Ingredients
Approx. 450g crab apples (about a dozen) or any other type
    of small apple
10 whole cloves
10 allspice berries (or 1tsp ground allspice)
2 cinnamon sticks
3l strong brown ale
450g soft dark brown sugar

1tbsp ground ginger
1tbsp ground nutmeg
700ml sweet sherry or 300ml calvados (or a half quantity
    of both)
6 eggs, separated (optional)

Materials and equipment: chopping board, knife, baking tray, cheesecloth, muslin or a tea filter bag, a length of string, a large saucepan, whisk, large mixing bowl and a wassail bowl or mugs

Method
1. Preheat the oven to 200°C /180°C fan/400°F/gas 6. Slice the crab apples in half and remove the core (try a metal piping tip rather than a regular apple corer, which is too large). Place them in a single layer on a baking tray and roast for about 30 minutes until soft.
2. While the crab apples are roasting, prepare the spices for infusion. Laying the cheesecloth, muslin or tea filter bag flat, add the cloves, allspice and cinnamon sticks and bring the edges together, tying tightly with string to create a parcel.
3. In a large pan, add the ale, sugar, ginger, nutmeg and spice parcel. Bring to the boil, then simmer gently for 20 minutes. Remove from the heat and add the sherry and/or calvados. Remove the spice parcel.
4. If you are adding the egg mixture, separate the yolks and egg whites and beat both (the whites until stiff peaks form) before recombining them. Add approx. 250ml of the hot liquid into the egg mixture (whisking gently as you pour). This tempers the egg mixture (so you are not consuming raw eggs) and prevents curdling. Now add the egg mixture to the hot liquid, stirring gently to combine. The froth will float to the surface.

5. Place the baked apples in a suitably large bowl and pour the hot mixture over them. Traditionally, wassail was drunk from a wassail bowl, passed between the celebrants, but of course it can be ladled into separate mugs, if you prefer.

Wassail! Wassail! All over the town,
our toast it is white and our ale it is brown;
our bowl it is made of the white maple tree;
with the wassailing bowl, we'll drink to thee.[5]

TREE OF THE MONTH

HAZEL

Shake and quiver, little tree,
Throw gold and silver down to me.[6]

Hazel catkins are among the earliest flowers to appear in the countryside, alongside winter aconite and snowdrop. Their tightly closed forms lengthen imperceptibly day by day. When their 'lamb's tails' appear, these waggling golden male flowers bring some cheer (despite spring being some time away). Look carefully along a branch and the diminutive female flowers will be found nearby, their bright red styles waiting to catch pollen.

The catkins are the tree's male sexual parts, while the separate female flowers have bright red feathery stigma to catch the pollen which the catkins release in the lightest breeze. It is easy to tell when the catkins are mature and releasing pollen by tapping your fingers against one (you will notice the powdery residue on your skin). Pollen-release happens before leaf-burst, so the new foliage does not limit the spread of pollen. Hazel pollen, like that of birch, is one of the main causes of hay fever in early spring.

Hazel was once one of our most productive woodland trees, and its vast range of uses led to large areas of hazel being managed in coppices (often called copses). Coppicing is a management technique which exploits hazel's ability to regenerate. The stems are cut close to the ground in winter. As the polymath John Evelyn wrote in 1664 in his influential forestry text *Sylva*, 'cut your trees near to the ground with a sharp bill [billhook], the moon decreasing', referring to the concept of tree tides (page 81). Sprouting from previously dormant buds under the bark of the stump, known as a hazel 'stool', multiple new shoots will appear in the spring. They are typically cut on a six- to nine-year cycle to produce straight rods or poles, which are used in a variety of ways, such as making fence hurdles or for wattle to support the daub for internal walls, in woven baskets, thatching spas, walking sticks (page 276) and more. Hazel also makes very good charcoal, which burned with a fierce heat useful in the iron foundries and lime kilns of the industrial revolution.

Over time, wildlife has adapted to living in hazel coppices, and their often light and airy conditions help nurture many woodland flowers and more than two hundred invertebrates. One of Britain's rarest (and cutest) mammals, the hazel dormouse, is only found in hazel woodlands. It is also found in Ireland where it is non-native, only discovered living in the wild within the last twenty years.

While hazel can be planted in new places, if a mature tree already exists it can also be easily propagated by layering. Take a reasonably long rod and bend it down to ground, and either peg it down or place something heavy enough on it to prevent it springing back. Where it touches the ground, it will soon grow roots, and after a short while it can be severed from its parent and transplanted.

Of course, hazel trees produce one of our favourite nuts, the hazelnut. Some varieties produce filberts, such as Cosford, Daviana and Merveille de Bollwiller, but other than their nuts, there are no biological differences between hazelnut, filbert and even another of its orchard and garden cousins, cobnut.

CELTIC TREE ZODIAC

Celtic astrology is based on a lunar calendar, which adopts the thirteen cycles of the Moon to comprise a year. The thirteen cycles of twenty-eight days combine to make up three hundred and sixty-four days, with a 'transition' or 'creation' day to complete the year. This was the calendar adopted by Ancient Britons and Celtic druids.

British poet Robert Graves (1895–1985) proposed the idea that each Moon cycle was linked to one of the sacred Celtic trees from the Early Medieval Ogham alphabet. It allows for the inclusion of bramble (sometimes named vine), ivy and reed, none of which actually qualify as trees by modern definition. Depending on when your birthday falls, you may find your character corresponds with the nature of one of the thirteen trees. You'll find descriptions of all thirteen included throughout the book.

CELTIC TREE ZODIAC

BIRCH	24th December–20th January
ROWAN	21st January–17th February
ASH	18th February–17th March
ALDER	18th March–14th April
WILLOW	15th April–12th May
HAWTHORN	13th May–9th June
OAK	10th June–7th July
HOLLY	8th July–4th August
HAZEL	5th August–1st September
BRAMBLE	2nd September–29th September
IVY	30th September–27th October
REED	28th October–24th November
ELDER	25th November–23rd December

BIRCH

24TH DECEMBER–20TH JANUARY

You are a pioneer, quick to grow and prosper. Your presence provides grace and beauty but you have great strength and tolerance. Your caring nature means that others near you always benefit and you are not unknown to sacrifice yourself for others. You like to be among others of your kind. Even in death, you provide homes and food for others. Compatible with Bramble and Willow.

ROWAN

21ST JANUARY–17TH FEBRUARY

Sometimes great things come in the smallest forms, and so it is for Rowan. You can light up any situation if you choose, though you often prefer a quiet and solitary life. You are able to persevere and succeed in situations few others can even imagine. Your resistance is legendary. Your spirit provides solace and protection to others. Compatible with Ivy and Hawthorn.

FEBRUARY

When the elm leaf is as big as a mouse's ear,
sow your barley without any fear.[7]

THE MONTH AHEAD

It is human nature to lend hope to the future, yet so much of our old folklore warns of over-optimism during the month of February. Winter may yet have a bite in its tail as snowfall, deep frosts, flooding and gales are all possible this month or next. Instead, simply enjoy any rare warm and sunny February days without allowing yourself to fantasise that spring has come! This is easier said and done, when nature agrees with you and flowers appear in our parks and woodlands, accompanied by birds singing in the trees.

February is a good month to complete work in the garden, orchard or forest – from maintaining tools, pruning and mulching, and even 'reading' your forest (page 43). Just remember that nature is waking up and this is the last month to complete some work before it's too late.

Birds are already looking for nesting sites, with some invertebrates becoming active on warm days. This month, a closer investigation is made of apterous moths, the characterful nuthatch, and the artful dodger of both town and country, the red fox.

You could collect cuttings of some trees and shrubs to bring indoors, where the artificial warmth will cause them to flower, bringing welcome colour to your home. Pussy willow, ornamental cherry, quince and witch hazel are all good candidates.

Elder is the tree of the month, providing perfect material for a making project: a traditional whistle with wonderful woody tones. Just remember that it's unlucky to bring elder indoors, whether to flower or even burn on a fire.

DATES OF NOTE

1 St Brigid's Day *(Imbolc) (bank holiday, ROI)*
2 Candlemas Day
7 Isra and Mi'raj
10 Lunar New Year
13 Shrove Tuesday *(Pancake Day)*
14 St Valentine's Day
14 Ash Wednesday
24 St Matthias's Day *(Patron saint of carpenters)*

OTHER SPECIAL EVENTS

CHINESE NEW YEAR (4721) begins on Saturday 10th February
(and ends on Tuesday 28th January 2025). In the Chinese
zodiac, 2024 is the year of the green wood dragon.

NATIONAL NESTBOX WEEK: a week of activities promoting
nestboxes to help breeding birds, held during the third
week of February.

MOON WOOD FELLING: 2nd–9th February.

PRACTICAL NOTES

IN THE GARDEN

The first bulbs may start appearing around the base of any trees in the garden (if not, make a mental note to plant some next autumn). If you are lucky to have some snowdrops growing, now is a good time to lift them 'green' (when in leaf) and plant them elsewhere to help them spread.

Ornamental shrubs such as any colourful varieties of dogwoods and willows should be pruned now by cutting all stems as low as possible to the ground. They will reward your efforts with vigorous and extra bright stems in the spring and summer.

Any shrubs that need to be moved can be dug up and lifted to their new positions, as long as the ground is not frozen. Make sure you leave as much of the rootball intact as possible.

Add circles of well-rotted compost to the base of fruit trees and shrubs, making sure you don't pile it up against the tree stem. If you have a shredder, mulch any cuttings and add them to your compost for next year.

While the garden is still dormant, now is a good time to

complete some maintenance on your tools. Wipe clean any cutting blades and rub with an oily cloth, lubricate moving parts and sharpen cutting blades.

IN THE FIELD AND ORCHARD

Pome fruit trees, like apple, pear and quince can be managed by giving them a 'winter prune'. Large branches and any branches which cross over others should be removed to prevent disease and to encourage growth of new fruiting wood (see branch pruning, page 259). Formative pruning can be undertaken to encourage a good framework of branches, allowing sunlight and air to reach the fruit. Don't prune stone-fruit trees, such as cherry and plum, as this can make them vulnerable to disease (see July, page 162). Walnut trees should also be left alone until the summer (page 162).

You could try your hand at propagating trees you admire in the orchard (see grafting, page 58). Take scionwood cuttings from the trees you want to propagate or 'graft' while they are still dormant. If you are not ready to use them immediately, place them in a bag wrapped in moist tissue and pop them in the fridge.

This is the latest time that hedges should be cut, trimmed or laid to avoid disturbing nesting birds.

IN THE FOREST

It is too late to be planting bare-root trees in the south of Britain or Ireland (page 15), but if you are using cell-grown or pot-grown trees then make the most of the thawing ground and less waterlogged soil to get your trees in the ground as soon as possible.

With broadleaved trees standing leafless in the forest, this is often a good time of year to 'read a woodland', or in other words, to assess its health and productivity. This requires some competency in identifying trees, which can be more of a challenge when they are leafless. However, their naked canopies allow full inspection of the trees' form and height. Foresters traditionally assess the trunk or stem of a tree by measuring its diameter 1.3m above the ground, which is called diameter at breast height (DBH) and is always given in centimetres. A diameter tape can be purchased, which automatically converts measured circumference to diameter in centimetres. By measuring enough trees in a woodland, it is possible to estimate the productivity of the woodland, expressed as the 'basal area'. Put together, all this information forms a woodland inventory.

If you are felling trees for timber, note that the moon wood period this month is 2nd–9th February (see Tree Tides, page 81).

SUN AND MOON

SUNRISE AND SUNSET

DATE	SUNRISE	SUNSET
1 FEBRUARY 2024, THURSDAY	8:06	16:56
2 FEBRUARY 2024, FRIDAY	8:04	16:58
3 FEBRUARY 2024, SATURDAY	8:03	17:00
4 FEBRUARY 2024, SUNDAY	8:01	17:02
5 FEBRUARY 2024, MONDAY	7:59	17:04
6 FEBRUARY 2024, TUESDAY	7:57	17:06
7 FEBRUARY 2024, WEDNESDAY	7:55	17:08
8 FEBRUARY 2024, THURSDAY	7:53	17:10
9 FEBRUARY 2024, FRIDAY	7:51	17:12
10 FEBRUARY 2024, SATURDAY	7:49	17:14
11 FEBRUARY 2024, SUNDAY	7:47	17:16
12 FEBRUARY 2024, MONDAY	7:45	17:18
13 FEBRUARY 2024, TUESDAY	7:43	17:20
14 FEBRUARY 2024, WEDNESDAY	7:41	17:22
15 FEBRUARY 2024, THURSDAY	7:39	17:24
16 FEBRUARY 2024, FRIDAY	7:37	17:26
17 FEBRUARY 2024, SATURDAY	7:35	17:28
18 FEBRUARY 2024, SUNDAY	7:33	17:30

19 FEBRUARY 2024, MONDAY	7:31	17:32
20 FEBRUARY 2024, TUESDAY	7:28	17:34
21 FEBRUARY 2024, WEDNESDAY	7:26	17:36
22 FEBRUARY 2024, THURSDAY	7:24	17:38
23 FEBRUARY 2024, FRIDAY	7:22	17:40
24 FEBRUARY 2024, SATURDAY	7:20	17:42
25 FEBRUARY 2024, SUNDAY	7:17	17:44
26 FEBRUARY 2024, MONDAY	7:15	17:46
27 FEBRUARY 2024, TUESDAY	7:13	17:48
28 FEBRUARY 2024, WEDNESDAY	7:10	17:50
29 FEBRUARY 2024, THURSDAY	7:08	17:52

* Sunrise and sunset times have been calculated for the centre of Britain and Ireland (a point just south of the Isle of Man).

FEBRUARY'S MOON PHASES

2 FEBRUARY	◗	*Third Quarter*
9 FEBRUARY	●	*New Moon*
16 FEBRUARY	◖	*First Quarter*
24 FEBRUARY	○	*Full Moon*

NOTABLES

9TH is a super new moon, when the Moon comes closest to Earth (technically known as its perigee). As for all new moons, it won't be visible, but this makes it a good time for night-sky gazing as it will be extra dark, helping even the faintest of stars and galaxies become more visible.

24TH is a full moon, traditionally known in Britain and Ireland as the Lenten moon. It is more commonly known today by the name used by Native American tribes – the snow moon – due to its coincidence with heavy snowfall. As its brightness made a successful night-hunt less likely, it was also known as a hunger moon.

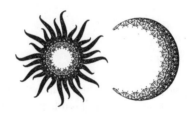

WILDLIFE

BIRDS

Many birds will start looking for mates and safe nesting places. It's not too late to erect a nestbox in your garden, just make sure that it is free from any coatings. If you can feed birds in your garden, it is important to keep doing so as they are now building up reserves in readiness for raising their young. Black sunflower seeds, peanuts and suet are particularly valuable as they are rich with protein and fats. One of the major fans of this range of food is the woodpecker-like nuthatch. With its blue-grey slate-coloured back, chestnut front and bold black stripe across its eye, this acrobatic bird is entertaining to watch. Nuthatches rarely fly outside woodland or parks and gardens with lots of trees. Their call is a short whistle with a rising pitch. They nest in natural tree holes or sometimes tit boxes, often plastering mud around the entrance to ensure it is tailor-made for the parents but difficult for predators to access.

Fieldfares and redwings are already departing Britain for Scandinavia after spending the winter months feeding on fruit and berries in our orchards and hedgerows.

One of the first moths to be seen each year is the distinctive herald moth. Its brown wings with orange blotches, criss-crossed with white lines, are scalloped along their margins. Adults spend the winter in outbuildings and barns before emerging in early spring. Their caterpillars feed on aspen, poplar and willow. Look for them near garden buildings and along hedgerows on sunny spring days.

Many moths which emerge at this time are apterous, meaning wingless, especially the females. Among these apterous species is the well-camouflaged spring usher, whose adults emerge this month and can be found resting on oak trunks. The pale brindled beauty is another type. The satellite moth is active all winter, named for its two bright spots on its otherwise brown and full wings.

Rising spring temperatures are a major trigger to frogs and toads to emerge from hibernation, having sheltered in old mammal burrows and under logs in woodlands and hedgerows (and garden compost heaps). In a warm February, it is quite likely that the first spawn will appear in ponds and the margins of other water bodies. Studies have shown that for every 1°C rise in temperature, the spawning date comes five days earlier. To search for frog and toad spawn, look just below the water's surface especially among water plants along the edges of ponds and ditches. As the temperature rises through the year, trees can help regulate the temperature of a pond, while their roots provide protection to tadpoles and other aquatic creatures.

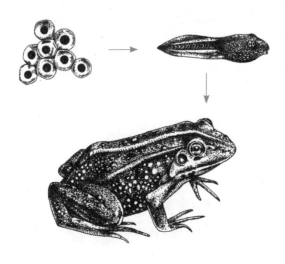

Red foxes are closely related to domestic dogs and are native to Britain and Ireland, being present everywhere except the Scilly Isles and Isle of Man, and absent from all Scottish islands except Harris and Skye. They have been hunted by humans for time immemorial, yet they are highly resilient and notorious for their cunning. Today, the estimated population is one-third of a million, but you are more likely to see one in a town or city than in the countryside. Urban areas in the south of Britain have the highest densities, the greatest being twenty-three foxes per km² in Bournemouth. In the countryside, they prey on voles, mice and in particular, rabbits. So much so that during the myxomatosis outbreak in the 1950s the population of red foxes reduced significantly. Red foxes also regularly dine on earthworms and recent declines in our fox population have been linked with the use of pesticides by gardeners and farmers. February is peak mating time for foxes, and the eerie screams of a female (vixen) heard in the middle of the night are unforgettable, and especially spine-tingling when echoing through a dark woodland.

PLANTS

Elder (our tree of the month, page 56) is one of the first trees to reach budburst each spring, starting as early as January in the south of Britain and Ireland, and more commonly from February. Budburst is the moment when the purple-tinged bud scales part to reveal emerging green leaves. If you are interested in studying the timing of budburst in trees – a science known as phenology – you could take part as a volunteer in the Woodland Trust's project Nature's Calendar (naturescalendar.woodlandtrust.org.uk).

One of the first insect-pollinated trees to flower each year is the cherry plum, whose white blossoms arrive months before blackthorn and hawthorn (discover more on page 129).

Sometimes known as 'February fair maids', snowdrops come into their own this month. Even when their pretty nodding heads are blanketed by snow or twinkling with hoar frost, they still bring a little cheer and warmth to the observer – spring is surely coming. Its Latin name, *Galanthus nivalis*, means 'milk flower of snow'. Even though it's a familiar charming winter flower, it is not native to Britain or Ireland, with the first record of it dating from 1597 and the first wild occurrence in Gloucestershire and Worcestershire in 1778. Snowdrops propagate by dividing their bulbs but also produce seed if there are insects flying between flowers. Hungry queen bumblebees emerging on sunny days are among the main pollinators. A naturally occurring substance extracted from snowdrops called galantamine is used to treat memory loss and dementia. Traditionally, snowdrops were considered a good medicine for headaches, but beware: the bulbs are poisonous if eaten.

TRADITION AND FOLKLORE

THE CELTIC FEAST OF IMBOLC
(1ST FEBRUARY)

Meaning 'in milk', the festival traditionally coincided with the start of lactation in sheep, goats and cows. It matched the arrival of young livestock and was the cause for great celebrations, signalling the imminent return of spring. Traditions often included the ceremonial pouring of milk onto the ground. Christians adopted the festival as Lá Fhéile Bríde or St Brigid's Day.

CANDLEMAS DAY

If Candlemas Day be fair and bright,
winter will have another flight,
but if it be dark with clouds and rain,
winter is gone and will not come again.[8]

Candlemas, on 2nd February, marks the return of light after a long winter, when candles are traditionally lit as a symbol of prosperity. It is a superstition that any Christmas tree not taken down by Twelfth Night in January should be left up until Candlemas.

The snowdrop, in purest white array,
First rears her head on Candlemas Day.[9]

ARTS AND CRAFTS

ELDER WHISTLE

The hollow pith of elder makes an ideal starter kit for a home-crafted whistle. Its resulting subtle woody tone is so much more elegant and unique than any modern plastic variety. I was taught this technique by my grandad, who was a champion Devon hedgelayer.

Materials and equipment: elder wood and a penknife

How to make
1. Choose and cut a suitable elder stem. It should measure about one finger length. Its thickness should be equivalent to an average thumb – thick enough to have a reasonable ring of wood around its soft hollow centre.
2. Peel off the bark. If the stick is green, push out the soft central pith, which will be present if using a small twig of the right diameter.
3. At the mouth end (you decide!), measure one knuckle's distance and make a vertical cut through the wood until you just reach the hollow inside.

4. Behind it, make a second cut at roughly a 45-degree angle to reach the base of the first cut. You have now cut out a 'frog'.

5. Whittle a plug to fill the hollow centre between the frog and the tip of the mouthpiece. Find a small green twig and carefully narrow it down so it will fit snugly into the hollow centre. Be careful that it's not too tight as it will split your nearly complete whistle. Don't push it in yet.

6. You need to provide a small gap for your breath to pass through. Carefully flatten the top side of your plug (only a couple of millimetres) before pushing it in. It should fit snugly and stay put without any glue.

7. Now you can test your whistle! You need to block the other end of it with your finger to successfully make a sound. If it sounds at all, then congratulations!

8. Now for some finishing touches. Using a similar small green twig, make another plug for the end so you don't need to use your finger. You can also carve a small amount away from the base of the mouthpiece so it's easier to fit between your lips.

FROG

MOUTHPIECE

TREE OF THE MONTH
ELDER

Make a fire of elder tree,
Death within your house will be.[10]

Elder is an intriguing small tree. At certain times of the year, it demands attention. In early summer its showy heads of creamy flowers hum with insects, while in the autumn its prominent clusters of dark purple berries (Englishman's grapes) are an important food source for birds. At other times of the year, it is quite innocuous.

Elder is intolerant of shade, so is not found deep within woodlands, but along ride edges and clearings. It is particularly successful growing on waste ground and in other places where few other trees thrive. It often grows as an epiphyte in the forks of big oak trees or among the resprouting stems of pollarded willows. Rabbits find it unpalatable so it can often be found near their warrens.

When young, elder stems are hollow, making them quite fragile. Those that break or are pruned back artificially create perfect hidey-holes for overwintering insects. In fact, a bundle of short cut stems hung up in the garden makes a wonderful bug hotel. Before plastic dominated our lives, elder stems made effective peashooters, whistles and drinking straws. The wood of old elder trees is solid right through, and its hard and tight grain was once much prized by watchmakers.

The popularity of drinks made from elderflowers has persisted in modern times, even while many equally good hedgerow recipes have faded. The fleeting delight (because it does not store well) of elderflower 'champagne' is justly famous and surprisingly easy to make (page 126). Insects are attracted in hordes to its flowers (which some people think smell of cat pee), particularly flies and longhorn beetles. Its berries are rich in vitamin C, and while they make fabulous jams and jellies, they're also loved by blackcaps, song and mistle thrushes, and starlings. They're often consumed in sufficient quantities to turn their droppings purple. As any scatologist (a person who studies poo) will know, the same droppings contain the undigested seeds of the elder, which is why the plant is so successful in spreading across our towns and countryside.

In winter, the distinctive fungus, variously known as jelly ear, wood ear or Judas's ear, is prominent on its stems. It is a popular fungus in Chinese medicine.

GRAFTING A FRUIT TREE

Propagating a tree by taking a cutting of it and joining it to the branches or roots of another may seem a mysterious dark art to be attempted only by those with the greenest fingers, but it is not as difficult as it may appear. Any such preconceptions should not prevent you from having a go at grafting. You will find that practice delivers more success!

You can add multiple different varieties of apple (or other fruit trees) to a single tree, so that each branch will yield different varieties of fruit from the same specimen (known as the 'rootstock'). The technique will work for many varieties within the same genus, in other words apple to apple, but it is difficult between those from a different genus (e.g. apple to pear). Ideally, your rootstock should be well-established (at least two years since planting).

The rootstock controls how large or tall the tree will grow, while the scion is responsible for fruit type, colour and flavour. So, the resulting growth is an exact copy of the original, in contrast to growing a tree from seed collected from your favourite tree, which would partly inherit the paternal genes (i.e. from pollen) from another tree.

To make a successful graft, you need to join the cambium of

the scion and rootstock together. The cambium is the layer of living tissue beneath the bark. There are many different joints or grafts that can be made, just like there are for joining wood when making a piece of furniture. The technique explained here is called the 'whip and tongue' method.

Materials and equipment: secateurs, grafting wax (or see method), grafting tape (or see method), sharp utility knife (i.e. use a new blade) or recently sharpened penknife

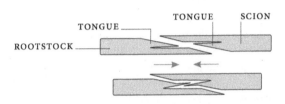

The scion and rootstock are pushed carefully together so the tongues on both interlock, as shown. The graft union is then bound tightly to prevent water loss and infection (see method).

Method

1. From your chosen variety, prepare to take cuttings ready to propagate, known as scionwood. If your friends or neighbours have varieties you like, you could ask their permission to collect some scionwood cuttings. The best time of year to collect these is when the trees are still dormant in late winter or early spring (e.g. January–early March), before the buds start to swell.
2. Choose branches which are less than a pencil thick in diameter, straight and free from any side branches. Trim to lengths which include no more than three buds.
3. You can keep scionwood for several weeks by wrapping in

moist tissue and placing in an airtight bag, before storing in the salad drawer of your fridge. Keep away from fruit in your fridge, which release a chemical (ethylene) that will kill the scionwood. If you collect from different rootstock varieties, make sure you label the different scionwood cuttings.

4. The best time to attempt a graft is when the buds on your rootstock tree are beginning to flush (open). When you are ready, keep the scionwood cuttings cool and out of sunlight when you take them outside. An insulated shopping bag is a good solution.

5. On the rootstock, choose a position where the branch is the same diameter as the scionwood. First make a long slanting cut with the knife, aiming for a cut surface 2–3cm long. Make a second cut into this to make a tongue (see illustration). Make sure you don't touch the exposed cambium as the oils in your hands will kill the exposed cells.

6. In the bottom of the scionwood, make a similarly long slanting cut with the knife. Again, make sure you don't touch the exposed cambium. Then cut into this surface to make a tongue.

7. Push the rootstock and scionwood together so that they interlock tightly. The cambium of each should now be connected.

8. Bind the graft union tightly. Grafting tape is the best material, but you can use other more common materials including raffia, strips of plastic bag, rubber bands or electrician's tape.

9. Seal the graft to prevent water loss and infection. Grafting wax is the best material but you can experiment with others. Children's modelling clay is quite effective. So too is cooling molten candle wax, but don't burn the sensitive graft union, or your fingers.

CELTIC TREE ZODIAC

ROWAN

21ST JANUARY–17TH FEBRUARY

Sometimes great things come in the smallest forms, and so it is for Rowan. You can light up any situation if you choose, though you often prefer a quiet and solitary life. You are able to persevere and succeed in situations few others can even imagine. Your resistance is legendary. Your spirit provides solace and protection to others. Compatible with Ivy and Hawthorn.

ASH

18TH FEBRUARY–17TH MARCH

With quiet strength and grace, your presence transcends the ordinary. You have an innate ability to heal hearts and minds, and bring others together. You are recognised as a leader among others, possessed with a sense of majesty, you are humble too. Undoubtedly a sunworshipper and given to be a little proud, sometimes your stature attracts the unkind. Yet you can flex and bend like any other, with the resilience to bounce back against the cruellest adversary. Compatible with Willow and Reed.

MARCH

*March winds and April showers
bring forth May flowers.*[11]

THE MONTH AHEAD

March is full of promise but can feel interminably long, stretching between the depths of winter and the burgeoning promise of spring. Our ancestors celebrated the spring equinox, which occurs this year on 20th March, with more verve than we do today, longing for the warmth of the Sun on their skin, the flowering of future crops and the birth of livestock.

This is the last month for many management activities in the garden or woodland to avoid disturbing breeding wildlife. The tree planting season is mostly over, tree pruning projects should be completed, while the first week of the month is the last chance to complete any moon wood felling. Regarding the Moon, there is a lunar eclipse on 25th March (page 71).

In the orchard this is the best time of year to propagate your favourite fruit varieties. Why not have a go yourself at grafting (page 58), using the scionwood collected earlier in the year? It is easier than you might imagine and a lot of fun.

Among the wildlife coming to life in March, bumblebees are worth a closer look in the garden or park. They will be hungry to feed on the 'first rose' of the year, the primrose, but daffodils provide more of a challenge because of their deep trumpets.

Perhaps you will spot one of the more recent new arrivals in Britain and Ireland, the tree bumblebee.

A spotlight is shone on the alder this month, a medium-sized tree which can be easily overlooked in the countryside, growing alongside waterways, and surrounding lakes and ponds in urban parks. Its curious seed heads, which look like miniature black cones when mature, provide the source for a fun activity making alder ink for writing or illustrating.

DATES OF NOTE

1   St David's Day *(Wales)*
8   Maha Shivaratri
10 Mother's Day
11 Ramadan begins
17 St Patrick's Day *(bank holiday observed in Ireland on 18th)*
20 Spring equinox
24 Palm Sunday
24 Purim
25 Holi
28 Maundy Thursday
29 Good Friday *(bank holiday, except ROI)*
31 Easter Sunday
31 daylight saving time begins *(clocks go forward)*

OTHER SPECIAL EVENTS

NATIONAL TREE WEEK: a week-long series of events during
    the last week of the month (ROI only).
MOON WOOD FELLING: 3rd–10th March.

PRACTICAL NOTES

IN THE GARDEN

If you haven't already done so, add some mulch to your trees and shrubs. If you have any flowering climbers like clematis and honeysuckle rambling over trees, now is a good time to cut them back to stimulate fresh growth and flowering. Clematis that flowers after June each year benefits from a harder prune (almost to ground level) than those which flower in spring and early summer.

This is a good time of year to build or install a compost heap if you don't already have one.

IN THE FIELD AND ORCHARD

With the increasing frequency of record-breaking warm years, horticulturists are concerned that many of our traditional apple varieties may begin to suffer, such as Cox's Orange Pippin and Egremont Russet. Many varieties require about one thousand chilling hours (below 6°C) each winter to thrive. Those from the southern hemisphere, like Gala which hails from New Zealand or Fuji from Japan, may prove more productive in a warming climate. However, as with many issues related to predicting the effects of climate change, it may not be as simple as that. Britain and Ireland are also projected to have wetter winters, and this may not favour some of these exotic varieties.

You can complete any grafting projects (page 58) this month. Wait for the buds on your rootstock plants to begin to flush.

Add mulch or well-rotted manure to the base of fruit trees in the orchard.

If you laid any hedgerows earlier in the year, enjoy watching them come into bud. Hopefully you will see signs of life emerging from the laid stems and tiny buds appearing on the stumps below the main cuts. Within weeks, the lattice work of stems and emerging shoots will create a solid barrier, protecting the land from wind and providing a safe corridor for wildlife to move through the landscape.

IN THE FOREST

This is the last month of the year to consider planting trees, certainly any bare-rooted trees (it's already too late if you are in the south of Britain, page 15), but less of an issue in Ireland). Trees planted later than March will require artificial watering if they are to survive, and even then, rarely thrive.

If you are felling trees for timber (page 81), note that the moon wood period this month is 3rd–10th March.

SUN AND MOON

SUNRISE AND SUNSET

DATE	SUNRISE	SUNSET
1 MARCH 2024, FRIDAY	7:06	17:54
2 MARCH 2024, SATURDAY	7:03	17:56
3 MARCH 2024, SUNDAY	7:01	17:58
4 MARCH 2024, MONDAY	6:59	18:00
5 MARCH 2024, TUESDAY	6:56	18:02
6 MARCH 2024, WEDNESDAY	6:54	18:04
7 MARCH 2024, THURSDAY	6:51	18:06
8 MARCH 2024, FRIDAY	6:49	18:08
9 MARCH 2024, SATURDAY	6:47	18:09
10 MARCH 2024, SUNDAY	6:44	18:11
11 MARCH 2024, MONDAY	6:42	18:13
12 MARCH 2024, TUESDAY	6:39	18:15
13 MARCH 2024, WEDNESDAY	6:37	18:17
14 MARCH 2024, THURSDAY	6:34	18:19
15 MARCH 2024, FRIDAY	6:32	18:21
16 MARCH 2024, SATURDAY	6:29	18:23
17 MARCH 2024, SUNDAY	6:27	18:25
18 MARCH 2024, MONDAY	6:25	18:27

19 MARCH 2024, TUESDAY	6:22	18:29
20 MARCH 2024, WEDNESDAY	6:20	18:30
21 MARCH 2024, THURSDAY	6:17	18:32
22 MARCH 2024, FRIDAY	6:15	18:34
23 MARCH 2024, SATURDAY	6:12	18:36
24 MARCH 2024, SUNDAY	6:10	18:38
25 MARCH 2024, MONDAY	6:07	18:40
26 MARCH 2024, TUESDAY	6:05	18:42
27 MARCH 2024, WEDNESDAY	6:02	18:44
28 MARCH 2024, THURSDAY	6:00	18:45
29 MARCH 2024, FRIDAY	5:57	18:47
30 MARCH 2024, SATURDAY	5:55	18:49
31 MARCH 2024, SUNDAY (DST BEGINS)	6:52	19:51

* Sunrise and sunset times have been calculated for the centre of Britain and Ireland (a point just south of the Isle of Man).

MARCH'S MOON PHASES

3 MARCH	◑	*Third Quarter*
10 MARCH	●	*New Moon*
17 MARCH	◐	*First Quarter*
25 MARCH	○	*Full Moon*

NOTABLES

20TH is the spring equinox, when the Sun shines directly on the equator and there are equal amounts of day and night. This also marks the first day of spring.

24TH Soon after sunset in the western sky, look for Mercury which will be at its highest point above the horizon in the evening sky.

25TH The full moon is commonly named the worm moon, marking the time when the ground thawed and earthworms reappeared. In Britain and Ireland, it is known as the egg moon.

25TH There will be a lunar eclipse visible at moonset, when the Moon falls under the Earth's shadow (penumbra).

WILDLIFE

BIRDS

March is the month when birdsong in our gardens, parks, orchards and woodlands reaches a peak among our resident birds. At this time of the year, our undisputed king of songbirds is the blackbird, although the song thrush is a close rival. Blackbird song includes a rich resonant tone alongside whistles, making it particularly beautiful to listen to on a spring morning. It is the male blackbird which more commonly sings, but during the breeding season females will occasionally sing in response to a male.

Brimstone butterflies are among the earliest to be seen flying each year across much of England and Wales, although they are seldom seen in Ireland or Scotland. The bright yellow males are quite easy to spot when flitting through a woodland glade or along a ride. The wings of females are a pale green. Both male and female can be hard to spot when perched, as their folded wings look like a tree leaf at springtime. Their larvae hatch during May and June to feed on the leaves of two species of shrubby trees: buckthorn and alder buckthorn.

Queen bumblebees can be seen on warm days, emerging from their hibernation holes underground to look for nest sites. Most bumblebees tend to nest under large logs, dense ground vegetation and abandoned mouse holes. It is a tough time for the queen who is busily focussed on starting a new colony while there is little nectar for her to feed on. Once her first clutch of eggs hatch into worker bees she then becomes sedentary, relying on them to feed her in the nest. Later in the year, she will produce males and new queens. The whole colony only lives for one year, even the queen, who'll be replaced by one of her offspring. You can help bumblebees in the garden by allowing clover and dandelion to flower, and by planting other early flowering species in the borders. Forest managers should always retain some areas of long grass and flowers along ride edges.

Tree bumblebees are now one of our eight most common species after arriving naturally as recently as 2001 in Britain and 2014 in Ireland. They are found across continental Europe, even as far north as the Arctic Circle. They are easy to identify with their thorax (the part behind the head where the wings are attached) being hairy and a bright ginger colour, while their abdomen is black with a white tip. They are among the most active bumblebees from March onwards, feeding on a wide range of flowers and trees including blackthorn and pussy willow, and later in the year on apple, pear and lime. Unlike most other bumblebees they like to nest above the ground, for example in tree hollows or bird boxes, especially those containing old bird nests. If you see a cloud of bees outside a bird nestbox, it is likely to be a group of tree bumblebees (bird nestboxes are too small for honeybees). Don't be alarmed, they won't swarm and are just flying together in a form of mating dance. If you can, try to leave a nest alone; the colony will come and be gone in just three to four months.

To find out more, go to the Bumblebee Conservation Trust: bumblebeeconservation.org.

MAMMALS

The usually solitary hare congregates in March to compete for territory and to breed. Hares can be seen boxing, standing on their back legs like champion prizefighters, usually a female attempting to dissuade an overly amorous male. Hares are usually seen on rough grassland or in arable fields. They also take advantage of young woodlands, enjoying the undisturbed open ground between the trees. Unfortunately for foresters, they also like to take a nip out of young tree seedlings in hedges and plantations, so the trees will need protecting up to 45cm above ground level using guards or tree shelters to prevent costly damage.

PLANTS

One of our most beautiful flowering plants, the primrose, heralds the arrival of spring in our woodlands, under trees in parks and in the undergrowth of hedgerows. It is especially beautiful seen growing on the raised hedgebanks of Devon, where it's recognised as the county flower. They are efficient seeders, spreading over time to create dense carpets of yellow. Their name was derived from *prima rosa,* meaning 'first rose' of the year, although they are not technically a member of the rose family. Wild forms are generally pale, creamy yellow with a golden centre, whilst the plant has been widely cultivated into thousands of varieties of primula. Environmentalists are concerned that hot, dry summers might lead to its decline, as seen in East Anglia in recent decades. Traditionally, the primrose symbolised youth and innocence.

> *When April laughed between her tears to see*
> *the early primrose with shy footsteps run*
> *from the gnarled oak-tree roots 'til all the wold,*
> *spite of its brown and trampled leaves, grew bright*
> *with shimmering gold.*[12]

TRADITION AND FOLKLORE

The wild daffodil, found growing in some of our ancient woodlands, is more dainty and shorter than the common cultivar. Its trumpet is always a strong golden hue, surrounded by a halo of paler yellow petals, and this two-tone colouration is quite distinct. It is also known as the 'Lent lily' because its flowers usually die before Easter.

The spring equinox falls on 20th March this year. Known as Alban Eilir among druids, it's marked as a time of balance, coming between the quiet of winter and the promise of summer, and halfway between Imbolc (page 52) and Bealtaine (page 124). Druids will celebrate the vibrancy of new life, of budburst and sap rising, and the arrival of energy and optimism.

ARTS AND CRAFTS

ALDER INK

Alder trees produce female flowers which look a little like cones (page 78), and can be used to make an excellent drawing or writing ink. The ink has a rich earthy hue which is light-fast too. You may not want to use the ink in your best fountain pen. Instead, use a dipping pen, or even experiment by making your own quill pen from any large feather you might come across in the park or countryside.

Materials and equipment: two handfuls of black (mature) alder 'cones', a saucepan, five cloves, muslin and small jam jars

How to make
1. Add the 'cones' to a pan with enough water to cover them. Add the cloves (which help act as a preservative).
2. Bring to the boil and simmer gently for 30 minutes until the water turns brown.
3. Strain the liquid through the muslin to remove any plant fragments.
4. When cool, decant into small jam jars and fix lids to prevent evaporation.

TREE OF THE MONTH
ALDER

The alder trees, the head of the line,
Formed the van.
The willows and quicken trees
Came to the army.[13]

Alder trees are thick with dangling catkins in February and March. Unlike those of hazel, which are bright golden yellow, the catkins of alder are darker. This colouration and the presence of its dark 'cones' is perhaps why our native alder is called black alder. It is most often found growing along the banks of rivers (where hazel is rare), making it easy to identify at this time of year.

The droopy catkins are the male flowers, while the female flowers start as clusters of green slightly pointed balls, becoming black as they mature. They look like the cones of a pine tree, but this is only in appearance as they are botanically unlike a coniferous cone. They open to release their seeds which are highly buoyant thanks to corky wings and air pockets, and perfectly adapted to be distributed by the water that they often overhang. In autumn, the seeds pods are popular among seed-eating birds, like siskin and redpoll.

Alder trees also grow in wet valley bottoms, fens and along the edges of marshy areas where it's an important tree, alongside willow, in creating 'carr' woodland – a special type of wet woodland rich in wildlife. There are concerns about the future of the species given projections for warming conditions under climate change. Sadly, alder is also affected by a soil-borne fungus, a type of Phytophthora, which can rapidly spread among trees along a riverbank.

Alder is not a large tree, growing to about 10m in height, and it does not tend to live for more than a few decades. It is a 'pioneer' species, like birch, being quick to grow in areas without trees, helping turn open ground into future forest. Like birch it is light-demanding and will soon die when overshadowed by larger trees that take over as the forest grows and matures.

Alder is rare among trees in being able to fix nitrogen, which is an atmospheric gas normally unavailable to plants. It has a bacterium (*Frankia alni*) that grows on its roots which works to help it capture the gas and make it available to the tree's roots. It forms visible nodules on the roots, which can be found by digging among the surface roots of almost every alder tree. This is a form of symbiotic relationship. The same process works in the roots of clover with another species of bacterium. Fortunately for other plants growing nearby, the soil is fertilised and made rich in nitrogen. The alder's leaves are also rich in nitrogen, so when these fall to the ground in autumn, they release more nitrogen into the soil. This is why foresters often include alder as a 'nurse' tree to help support other young trees in new plantations, particularly in poor soils.

Alder is not a widely used timber, although it has many useful properties. It is sometimes used for mouldings (e.g. skirting boards) and plywood but is rarely available in sufficient quantities. One of its niche uses was once for clog making. More famously today, it is the wood of choice for the body of electric guitars, especially Fender guitars, as it is lightweight but highly resonant. Its cones can be used to make an ink (page 77).

The most highly prized charcoal for gunpowder manufacture was once made from alder. Capable of being coppiced, alder could be cut repeatedly, and its rapidly growing stems harvested for the industry. Today, scientists are interested in the tree because it contains a wide range of beneficial properties that have been used in medications, including in cancer treatments.

TREE TIDES

Most of us are aware that the Moon exerts a force on our oceans, causing a bulge in water levels (high tides) when it is nearest any particular area of the planet. In some places, water can rise as much as 10m or more. This happens twice every period lasting 24 hours and 50 minutes.

Twice every month, the Earth lines up with the Sun and the Moon. When Sun and Moon are together on the same side, the presence of both celestial bodies together creates a maximum gravitational force on the Earth. At this time, the Moon is in full shadow and appears dark; in other words, it is a new moon. When all three celestial bodies are in alignment, but the Earth is between Sun and Moon, then the Moon is in full sunlight, in other words it is a full moon. In both cases (new moon or full moon), the alignment of the three celestial bodies creates the highest tides, known as spring tides (despite their name they have nothing to do with the season and occur twice every month throughout the year).

Water in any place, including inside plants, may also be affected by these gravitational forces. Known as tree tides, they can affect trees in several ways including their quantities of stored water, stem diameter and seed germination. People have been fascinated with the notion that time of year matters when it comes to felling a tree because it affects timber quality. The timber was thought to be particularly strong and hard-wearing if felled in the period between a waning moon and a new moon. Our ancestors were convinced, including Julius Caesar, and famed natural philosopher Pliny the Elder.

Scientists today are still unsure, but one study revealed that wood harvested during the waning moon, known as moon wood, has more water stored in its vessels. This meant that it shrunk less during the drying process, being denser, more resistant to compression, and more durable to fungal decay.

In summary, tree felling should be undertaken between the time that leaf-fall starts and when new tree growth begins, i.e. during a waning moon or new moon.

During 2024, the best times for tree felling are:

4TH–11TH JANUARY
2ND–9TH FEBRUARY
3RD–10TH MARCH
24TH OCTOBER–1ST NOVEMBER
23RD NOVEMBER–1ST DECEMBER
22ND–30TH DECEMBER

CELTIC TREE ZODIAC

ASH

18TH FEBRUARY–17TH MARCH

With quiet strength and grace, your presence transcends the ordinary. You have an innate ability to heal hearts and minds, and bring others together. You are recognised as a leader among others, possessed with a sense of majesty, you are humble too. Undoubtedly a sunworshipper and given to be a little proud, sometimes your stature attracts the unkind. Yet you can flex and bend like any other, with the resilience to bounce back against the cruellest adversary. Compatible with Willow and Reed.

ALDER

18TH MARCH–14TH APRIL

Your fondness of the aquatic is well known. You are a generous provider of gifts and food, selflessly taking pleasure in sustaining those around you. In fact, those in your circle tend to benefit from good luck and prosperity. You have a rare talent for understanding different points of view, with an uncanny ability to ward off the unpleasant and evil. At your heart, you are more durable than any other. Compatible with Hawthorn and Oak.

APRIL

Ash before oak, we're in for a soak
Oak before ash, then only a splash.[14]

THE MONTH AHEAD

Life is bursting forth this month, with our songbirds in full voice and plants growing at an incredible rate. Most of our trees will be flushing (leaves expanding from buds), except walnuts and a few other species. Those that come into leaf late are often sensitive to frost, so gardeners and growers will be anxious for no late frosts in April, let alone into early May.

It's a quiet time for tree care, except for mulching trees in the garden or orchard. If you tried your hand at grafting last month, you will be excited to see whether your grafts have 'taken'. If they didn't, don't despair, there's always next year.

Look out for a partial solar eclipse early in the month. If you can be outside when it occurs, pay attention to wildlife, and observe how it responds – you may even witness a 'false' dawn chorus. Tree leaves also do a great job at focussing the Sun's rays, just like a pinhole camera, allowing you to observe the solar event safely by looking at the amazing multiple crescents in the shape of the light and shadows cast under a tree. This is particularly evident below street trees on the smooth pale surfaces of pavements and patios.

Whether they fascinate or repel, we celebrate the three

snakes native to Britain which you may be lucky enough to spot emerging.

This month, a craft project for aspiring artists and woodlanders alike is to make homemade drawing charcoal. Perhaps you could have a go drawing our queen of trees, the ash, which is in the spotlight this month. As one of our most common broadleaved trees, both conservationists and the general public are watching anxiously to see whether it manages to overcome a devasting new pathogen, unlike the English elm which all but died out in the 1970s. Scientists however are working on breeding disease-resistant ash trees, taking samples from the 5 per cent of the population which appear to have some natural resistance.

DATES OF NOTE

 1 Easter Monday *(bank holiday)*
 5 Laylatul Qadr
10 Eid al-Fitr
23 First day of Passover
23 St George's Day *(England)*
23 Shakespeare Day
30 Last day of Passover

OTHER SPECIAL EVENTS

ORCHARD BLOSSOM DAY: a weekend of events centred around the end of April.

PRACTICAL NOTES

IN THE GARDEN

Finish moving any shrubs and planting trees in the garden before they become too active. As it is now quite late in the season, you may need to water them if there is a dry spell. It's not too late to add a layer of well-rotted compost or manure as a mulch around the base of trees or shrubs.

If a late-spring frost is forecast, you can help limit damage to the blossoms of fruit trees by covering them with horticultural fleece.

IN THE FIELD AND ORCHARD

If you haven't done so already, mulch your fruit trees with well-rotted compost and/or manure, avoiding piling any against the tree stem. As in the garden, beware of late-spring frosts and be prepared to protect the blossoms of fruit trees. If you have any recently planted trees, resist the urge to allow them to blossom as the energy required to produce fruits is much better invested in growing roots and shoots, and in helping the tree become well established. Also, their young slender branches are more likely to be overcome by the weight of any fruit. Be brave and remove any blossoms by pinching them off.

If you completed any grafting, you will be anxiously waiting to see if your scionwood cuttings (page 58) are still alive and that the graft has been successful. Watching new shoots successfully emerging from the scionwood is very satisfying.

IN THE FOREST

Keep an eye on any recently planted areas, especially if you have used tree shelters. Strong winds can often result in leaning stakes and shelters, especially when the ground is soft immediately after planting. Don't allow rapidly growing weeds to overcome young trees.

SUN AND MOON

SUNRISE AND SUNSET

DATE	SUNRISE	SUNSET
1 APRIL 2024, MONDAY	6:50	19:53
2 APRIL 2024, TUESDAY	6:47	19:55
3 APRIL 2024, WEDNESDAY	6:45	19:57
4 APRIL 2024, THURSDAY	6:43	19:58
5 APRIL 2024, FRIDAY	6:40	20:00
6 APRIL 2024, SATURDAY	6:38	20:02
7 APRIL 2024, SUNDAY	6:35	20:04
8 APRIL 2024, MONDAY	6:33	20:06
9 APRIL 2024, TUESDAY	6:30	20:08
10 APRIL 2024, WEDNESDAY	6:28	20:10
11 APRIL 2024, THURSDAY	6:26	20:11
12 APRIL 2024, FRIDAY	6:23	20:13
13 APRIL 2024, SATURDAY	6:21	20:15
14 APRIL 2024, SUNDAY	6:19	20:17
15 APRIL 2024, MONDAY	6:16	20:19
16 APRIL 2024, TUESDAY	6:14	20:21
17 APRIL 2024, WEDNESDAY	6:12	20:23
18 APRIL 2024, THURSDAY	6:09	20:25

19 APRIL 2024, FRIDAY	6:07	20:26
20 APRIL 2024, SATURDAY	6:05	20:28
21 APRIL 2024, SUNDAY	6:02	20:30
22 APRIL 2024, MONDAY	6:00	20:32
23 APRIL 2024, TUESDAY	5:58	20:34
24 APRIL 2024, WEDNESDAY	5:56	20:36
25 APRIL 2024, THURSDAY	5:53	20:38
26 APRIL 2024, FRIDAY	5:51	20:39
27 APRIL 2024, SATURDAY	5:49	20:41
28 APRIL 2024, SUNDAY	5:47	20:43
29 APRIL 2024, MONDAY	5:45	20:45
30 APRIL 2024, TUESDAY	5:43	20:47

* Sunrise and sunset times have been calculated for the centre of Britain and Ireland (a point just south of the Isle of Man).

APRIL'S MOON PHASES

2 APRIL	◐	*Third Quarter*
8 APRIL	●	*New Moon*
15 APRIL	◑	*First Quarter*
23 APRIL	○	*Full Moon*

NOTABLES

8TH A partial solar eclipse may be briefly visible in western Britain and Ireland as the Sun sets.

22ND–23RD The Lyrid meteor shower, producing up to twenty meteors per hour, may be visible overnight. They will radiate from the Lyra constellation but could be seen in any part of the night sky.

23RD A full moon, known as the milk moon, may be seen in Britain and Ireland.

WILDLIFE

BIRDS

Nightingales arrive from April. They are found in only localised sites in the south of Britain, mostly between Dorset in the west to East Anglia, Kent and Sussex in the east, and are even rarer in Ireland. They are extremely secretive and like to habit, sing and nest in the thickest and most impenetrable scrub and thicket, particularly of blackthorn and alder buckthorn. Together with their plain buff plumage, this makes them very difficult to see. Their song however is unmistakable and can be heard from late April to June. None of our other birds can rival the complex and varied song of the nightingale, which once heard is never forgotten. If you are keen to hear one, in Britain the RSPB reserves of Blean Woods, Highnam Woods and Wolves Wood are worth visiting in late May and June.

Thou wast not born for death, immortal Bird![15]

April is the start of the best period of the year to listen to the dawn chorus. Make a special effort to get up early one morning (ideally when not wet and windy) about 30 minutes before sunrise, to catch the whole chorus. It starts subtly with just a few birds, before a gradual crescendo begins with more and more birds joining in. Blackbird, robin and song thrush are early starters, while warblers and wren seem to prefer a lie-in, starting later during the second or third movement! There are other birds to listen out for beyond the songbirds. The distinctive husky 'hoo-hroo' of wood pigeon can often be heard in the background. You may be lucky enough to hear a cuckoo calling, newly arrived after its migration from Africa. Cuckoos are now considered a high conservation priority after steep declines in their breeding population.

INVERTEBRATES

Among our butterflies that hibernate over winter, April is the time when many emerge to feed on early flowering plants. Look for green-veined white, red admiral, small tortoiseshell and peacock. Another common species seen along woodland edges, rides and hedgerows is the orange-tip. Only the male has the easy-to-spot orange wingtips which add colour to this otherwise white butterfly. Its caterpillars feed on a range of plants, including cuckoo flower, and are hard to spot. They are cannibals, often eating those of their own kind they come across!

REPTILES

There are three species of snake native to Britain, but none are present in Ireland. The increasing warmth of April encourages native snakes to wake from hibernation. The longest, and completely harmless, is the grass snake, which will spend the winter under logs or in abandoned animal burrows before emerging in April. It favours wetland habitats, especially wet grasslands, and ponds. It is also fond of compost heaps in the garden. It can live up to twenty-five years.

Britain's only venomous snake, the adder, also emerges in April and is more likely to be seen in woodland and heathland habitats. Unlike the grass snake, adders give birth to live young. They are found across the whole of Britain except for the Isles of Scilly. Adders are shy and will disappear on the sound of an approaching person and will not attack people or dogs unless provoked (accidentally or deliberately). Bites are rare in Britain, and its poison generally only causes painful inflammation except for vulnerable people (young, old or those with existing medical conditions). If bitten, however, medical attention should be sought immediately. Adders use their venom to hunt for lizards, small mammals, and the chicks of ground-nesting birds.

Another native snake in Britain, which looks like the adder but without the distinctive black zigzag pattern along its back, is the smooth snake. It is rare in Britain, found only in a few places with sandy heathland. It is a constrictor species, coiling around its prey to suffocate it.

Some people may think the slow worm might be included as a fourth species of snake, but it is neither a snake nor a worm, but a legless lizard! Unlike true snakes, it is found in Ireland (though infrequently), and only in County Clare and County Galway.

If you are keen to spot a snake, early morning is a good time – when they emerge from night-time shelter to absorb the early rays of the Sun. Walk quietly and if you are lucky enough to spot one, keep a respectful distance away. All snakes in Britain are protected by law, their number declining rapidly due to loss of habitat.

MAMMALS

All eighteen native species of bat will emerge this month, ravenous after a long hibernation. Each bat can consume thousands of invertebrates each night, and so are heavily reliant on habitats which support good populations of flying invertebrates. Ponds and open grassy glades in woodlands are particularly important for bats, and worth visiting at dusk to watch bats emerging from the trees. Within woodland, standing deadwood provides sites for hibernation and shelter, and are also rich in invertebrates. Honeysuckle can be encouraged to grow alongside ride edges, being a particularly good source of nectar for invertebrates. Once bats have replenished their reserves, they will be ready to mate in May.

Bluebell flowers carpet the ground of woodlands during April and May, particularly ancient woodlands which have been undisturbed for centuries. They arise from bulbs in the soil, their bright green leafy blades first appearing in March, before flooding our woodlands with colour. The nodding heads of bluebells attract many pollinating insects, providing a valuable source of nectar in return. Bumblebees have trouble reaching inside the flower and will nibble a hole through the petals. They are a common plant, while certain sites become well known for having particularly spectacular carpets of flowers each spring. In Britain, the Wildlife Trusts have a guide to sites: wildlifetrusts.org/where_see_bluebells.

While bluebells may captivate you, don't forget to spot other spring flowers that often grow alongside bluebells in ancient woodlands. One of the most common is ramsons, also known as wild garlic for the distinctive smell when its leaves are crushed. Its pretty white clusters of flowers can also carpet the ground of woodlands from April onwards.

TRADITION AND FOLKLORE

The fertility goddess Eostre was so popular among pagans that early Christians didn't change the festival's name when it was absorbed. It did however change from a three-day orgy into the Christian festival of Easter, celebrated around much of the world on the first Sunday after the first full moon that occurs on or after the spring equinox.

Traditionally, it was thought the cuckoo (page 120) called from St Tiburtius's Day (14th April) until St John's Day (24th June):

> *In April I open my bill,*
> *in May I sing night and day,*
> *in June I change my tune,*
> *in July far far I fly,*
> *in August away I must.*[16]

GUARDIAN TREES OF THE
FIVE PROVINCES

According to folklore in Ireland, a stranger as tall as the trees themselves entered the court of the high king at Tara. He carried a single branch which bore three fruits: apple, acorn and hazelnut. He was named Trefuilngid Tre-eochair, meaning 'of the three sprouts'.

Trefuilngid Tre-eochair taught the wisest people in the land everything he knew of trees, about their history, utility and nature. With his mission complete, he passed the fruits of the miracle branch to an ancient wise man, who cultivated their seeds and planted the young five seedlings across the country. One was planted at its centre, the others one in each quarter. All of these prospered in the country's fertile land and grew into great trees known as the Five Sacred Trees or the Guardian Trees of the Five Provinces.

One of the five sacred trees was a yew tree, another an oak and the remaining three were ash trees:

The Yew of Rossa (Eó Ruis) stood at Old Leighlin, County Carlow.

The Mighty Oak (Eó Mugna) grew at Ballaghmoon, County Kildare. This was the only tree which inherited the ability to grow three fruits on a single branch.

The three ash trees were the Tree of Tortu (Bile Tortan), near Navan in County Meath; the Branching Tree of Daithe (Craeb Daithí) at Farbill, County Westmeath; and the third, Craeb Uisnig, stood at the centre of the provinces.

The trees were revered for their long lives and it was believed their roots connected with the underworld.

ARTS AND CRAFTS

ARTIST'S DRAWING CHARCOAL

Botticelli, da Vinci and Van Gogh are just a few among many famous artists to use charcoal in their art. More contemporary examples include the German artist Käthe Kollwitz (1867–1945) and the American modernist artist Georgia O'Keeffe (1887–1986). It is easy to buy charcoal from an art shop, but it is also quite easy to make at home. Using a material made with your own hands adds to the satisfaction of any finished work of art.

Charcoal is made by heating wood to at least 400°C in an atmosphere without any oxygen. There is less alchemy involved than you might think, and with a little ingenuity and a hot fire it is quite simple. It's a great activity to do with children, provided you take appropriate precautions to avoid danger from burns or cuts.

Willow makes the finest drawing charcoal, although almost all wood can be used. Other popular wood is spindle (which grows very straight) and even the prunings off vine plants. It is important that the bark is stripped off before processing, and for this reason making charcoal is a little easier when the sap is rising in the spring and when the bark is green. Sticks make better charcoal if dried out a little before being 'cooked', so if you can, keep them inside somewhere warm for twenty-four hours.

Materials and equipment: twigs or sticks of about pencil-thickness (smaller diameters are easier to make); tinfoil or a recycled metal tin (e.g. a biscuit or chocolate tin), secateurs and a source of intense heat (e.g. a barbecue or open fire)

How to make

1. Cut the sticks to a consistent length of about 10cm (or the right size to fit the foil or tin).
2. Peel off all bark from the sticks – they make better charcoal if allowed to dry out a little, for example by keeping inside a warm house for 24 hours. Prepare the sticks for heating. If using foil, place about six sticks together and wrap them very tightly in the foil, ensuring that at least four layers of foil surround them and that all edges are completed sealed with multiple folds. If using a tin, fill it to the brim with sticks (they will shrink by about 50 per cent in volume) and place the lid on securely, using wire to keep it from popping off in the extreme heat.
3. Place your foil bundle or tin into the heat source – flames should be avoided, so either use a barbecue that has subsided or the hot coals in the base of an open fire.
4. Leave it in the fire for twenty-four hours or until all heat has dissipated (the slower the 'cook', the better the charcoal), before attempting to open.
5. If successful, you should have a lovely collection of drawing charcoal which will be ready to use for your art. If you notice any brown patches on the sticks, then sadly your fire was not hot enough. Don't despair as you can reseal the bundle or tin and try again without needing to start from scratch.

TREE OF THE MONTH
ASH

*Ash new or ash old
is fit for a queen with a crown of gold.*[17]

In recent years, or more precisely since 2012, the plight of common ash has become well known with the arrival of ash dieback disease. Symptoms include wilting leaves, necroses and cankers on stems and branches, followed by severe leaf loss and dieback of the tree canopy. It is caused by a pathogenic fungus, *Hymenoscyphus fraxineus*. Although first spotted in Britain and Ireland in 2012, it had already been prevalent among our ash for years, if not decades before, but simply unnoticed. Once it came to the notice of the public, the immediate fear was that the disease could mark the loss of another iconic tree in an already tiny list of native species (page 205), especially given the loss of English elm in the 1970s. Since then, although the disease is certainly decimating, there are pockets of resistance, and the spread of the disease is slower than anticipated. There is hope, too, in that there is good evidence of natural resistance among a small (around 5 per cent) population of our ash trees.

This month and into May, its buds will be flushing (leaves emerging) and the first shoots expanding. Is there any truth in the old weather lore (page 85) about whether ash comes into leaf before or after oak, and how that will determine how wet the summer will be? Scientific studies (often with the help of volunteers) tell us that both ash and oak are flushing earlier today than they were in the past, but the jury is out when it comes to the significance of which tree is first to flush in any year. It is worth keeping a note and coming to your own conclusions, or better still get involved in a citizen science project like the Woodland Trust's Nature's Calendar (www.woodland-trust.org.uk) or Treezilla (www.treezilla.org). Keep a close eye on the young shoots of ash as they are particularly vulnerable to dieback – any that show signs of wilting will be infected.

Ash has long been valued as one of our most productive hardwoods, growing relatively quickly in about seventy years to produce high-quality timber. Its pale wood makes it perfect for a wide range of uses, from large furniture to small wooden boxes. Sometimes the heart of ash is coloured dark brown, which is much loved in the trade and marketed as 'olive ash'. The timber of ash is also extremely flexible and strong for its weight. It has traditionally been used for tennis rackets and hockey sticks. The Irish games of camogie and hurling have always demanded ash for their hurley sticks (camán in Irish) and these are cut from the very base of a tree and from the top of the roots, using the natural curve and strength of this area to produce the distinctive profile. Even the by-products of all these many uses are valued, especially the quality of ash for firewood.

Ash is a light-demanding tree, so you will not find it growing under the heavy shade of oaks or various conifers. Nor does it like cold hollows, being sensitive to late-spring frosts. It thrives along the sunny edges of woodland clearings and rides, and is especially elegant as a standard tree in a hedgerow and as a specimen tree in large gardens and parks. It produces winged seeds, known as a samara, which tend to stay fast on the trees until the end of winter before being disseminated by the wind. It is quite easy to identify – in winter, look for its dark olive-green buds which are arranged in opposite pairs. When in leaf, notice that it has compound leaves consisting of seven–eleven leaflets arranged in opposite pairs except the very last which is a single leaflet.

Beech wood fires burn bright and clear,
if the logs are kept a year.
Oaken logs burn steadily,
if the wood is old and dry.
But ash dry or ash green,
makes a fire fit for a queen.

Logs of birch wood burn too fast,
there's a fire that will not last!
Chestnut's only good, they say,
if for long it's laid away.
But ash new or ash old,
is fit for a queen with a crown of gold!

Poplar makes a bitter smoke,
fills your eyes and makes you choke!
It is by the Irish said,
hawthorn bakes the sweetest bread.
But ash green or ash brown,
is fit for a queen with a golden crown.

Elm wood burns like churchyard mould,
even the very flames are cold.
Apple logs will fill your room,
with an incense-like perfume.
But ash wet or ash dry,
is fit for a queen to warm her slippers by![18]

FROM THE FOREST TO
THE STARS

The mythical goddess of the hunt, forests and all things wild was known as Artemis among the Ancient Greeks (and Diana by the Romans). She had a number of devoted nymphs, among them Callisto, whose name means 'most beautiful'. Callisto swore an oath of chastity to her leader but was later tricked (some say raped) by the supreme god Zeus, who had disguised himself as Artemis. She became pregnant and gave birth to a son, Arcas. In fury, Zeus's wife, Hera, turned poor innocent Callisto into a bear.

Many years later, when Arcas had grown up, he went hunting in the forest. Spotting a great bear among the trees he took aim with his spear. Of course, he didn't realise that the bear was his mother. Luckily, and just in time, Zeus intervened and saved his life. He decided to grant Callisto eternal life by placing her and their son in the heavens as a constellation of stars.

Ursa Major, as we now call the great she-bear, is always visible, but the best time to see her is in the spring when she is at her highest above the north-east horizon. The Plough (or saucepan) makes up the hindquarters and tail of the bear, but the remainder of the constellation is dimmer, and a dark sky is needed to see it clearly.

We use the line of the two stars which make up the right-hand side of the Plough or the pan part of the saucepan (known as the 'pointer stars' called Merak and Dubhe), to point to our most important star in the night sky, namely the North Star.

We now know the little bear (Arcas) as Ursa Minor. The North Star is found at the tip of the little bear's tail.

CELTIC TREE ZODIAC

ALDER

18TH MARCH–14TH APRIL

Your fondness of the aquatic is well known. You are a generous provider of gifts and food, self-lessly taking pleasure in sustaining those around you. In fact, those in your circle tend to benefit from good luck and prosperity. You have a rare talent for understanding different points of view, with an uncanny ability to ward off the unpleasant and evil. At your heart, you are more durable than any other. Compatible with Hawthorn and Oak.

WILLOW

15TH APRIL–12TH MAY

You are the spirit of any place, graceful, lithe and ever youthful in body and mind. Highly sociable, you are quick to adapt to a situation and comfortable in the company of others. You have an innate ability to bind parts together, weaving strength and protection into every situation. When you choose to, you blossom like no other, attracting whispers of admiration from the wind. Compatible with Birch and Ivy.

MAY

When the glow-worm lights her lamp,
then the air is always damp.[19]

THE MONTH AHEAD

Our dawn chorus is made up of dozens of different birds in full song and is spectacular. It is celebrated during International Dawn Chorus Day on the first Sunday of the month. Towards the end of the month, Oak Apple Day in the UK celebrates an event which occurred more than four hundred years ago.

This month, the full moon is known as the flower moon. In the garden and orchard, fruit trees are in full bloom, and bees, flies and other flying invertebrates are doing their best to feed on the glut of nectar, unknowingly pollinating the flowers. If you have a lawn, consider allowing it to grow longer to provide habitat for precious invertebrates, or lobby your local council to leave the verges alone during 'No Mow May'.

Both in Ireland and Great Britain, keep an eye out for a variety of resident dragonfly species and the closely related damselflies. Two tree species focussed on this month rely on invertebrates to reproduce. One is hawthorn (also known as maythorn), while elder provides us with the classic country tipple of elderflower 'champagne'.

DATES OF NOTE

3 Orthodox Good Friday
4 Orthodox Holy Saturday
5 Orthodox Easter
6 Yom HaShoah *(Holocaust Remembrance Day)*
6 Orthodox Easter Monday
6 May Day *(Bealtaine) (ROI only)*
6 Early May bank holiday
9 Ascension Day
13 First day of Yom Ha'atzmaut
19 Pentecost
20 Whit Monday
26 Trinity Sunday
26 Lag B'Omer
27 Late May spring bank holiday *(except ROI)*
29 Oak Apple Day
30 Corpus Christi

5TH International Dawn Chorus Day.

NATIONAL GARDENING WEEK: activities in the UK for all gardeners during the first week of May.

NATIONAL HEDGEROW WEEK: celebrating the beauty of hedges and the craft of hedgelaying during the second week of May in the UK.

NATIONAL WALNUT DAY: mostly celebrated in the USA, the beauty and utility of walnut trees are celebrated on 17th May.

PRACTICAL NOTES

IN THE GARDEN

Some shrubs which flower in early spring can be pruned when flowering is over. If you have clumps of daffodils or other bulbs surrounding the base of trees, now is a good time to lift and divide them to help them spread where you want them to grow more.

IN THE FIELD AND ORCHARD

May is a glorious month in the orchard, with fruit trees in full bloom. Among the showy white and blushing blossom, don't overlook the wind-pollinated trees. Walnut trees produce chunky male catkins which are bright green, while its female flowers are like miniature urns which quickly begin to swell once fertilised.

If you have young, staked trees, check the ties to ensure they have not become over-tight as the trees grow. Make sure that the stake has been effective in preventing its rootball being rocked by high winds, checking for gaps around the roots and compacting the soil with your heel.

Hopefully, anyone managing a garden lawn, orchard, park or forest ride will consider observing 'No Mow May'. Leaving grasses and flowering plants to grow taller and to come to flower can have a massive beneficial impact on wildlife.

IN THE FOREST

Now is not the time to undertake any active management in the forest, with wildlife of all sorts in full breeding mode. However, this makes it a good time to sit back and watch wildlife thrive. If you have any nestboxes erected, consider working with local bird-ringing groups who may be interested in helping monitor chick mortality, fledging dates, and in ringing the young birds in the hope they will help the scientific community learn more about woodland and wild bird populations.

SUN AND MOON

SUNRISE AND SUNSET

DATE	SUNRISE	SUNSET
1 MAY 2024, WEDNESDAY	5:41	20:49
2 MAY 2024, THURSDAY	5:39	20:50
3 MAY 2024, FRIDAY	5:37	20:52
4 MAY 2024, SATURDAY	5:35	20:54
5 MAY 2024, SUNDAY	5:33	20:56
6 MAY 2024, MONDAY	5:31	20:58
7 MAY 2024, TUESDAY	5:29	21:00
8 MAY 2024, WEDNESDAY	5:27	21:01
9 MAY 2024, THURSDAY	5:25	21:03
10 MAY 2024, FRIDAY	5:23	21:05
11 MAY 2024, SATURDAY	5:21	21:07
12 MAY 2024, SUNDAY	5:19	21:08
13 MAY 2024, MONDAY	5:18	21:10
14 MAY 2024, TUESDAY	5:16	21:12
15 MAY 2024, WEDNESDAY	5:14	21:13
16 MAY 2024, THURSDAY	5:13	21:15
17 MAY 2024, FRIDAY	5:11	21:17
18 MAY 2024, SATURDAY	5:09	21:18

19 MAY 2024, SUNDAY	5:08	21:20
20 MAY 2024, MONDAY	5:06	21:22
21 MAY 2024, TUESDAY	5:05	21:23
22 MAY 2024, WEDNESDAY	5:04	21:25
23 MAY 2024, THURSDAY	5:02	21:26
24 MAY 2024, FRIDAY	5:01	21:28
25 MAY 2024, SATURDAY	5:00	21:29
26 MAY 2024, SUNDAY	4:58	21:31
27 MAY 2024, MONDAY	4:57	21:32
28 MAY 2024, TUESDAY	4:56	21:34
29 MAY 2024, WEDNESDAY	4:55	21:35
30 MAY 2024, THURSDAY	4:54	21:36
31 MAY 2024, FRIDAY	4:54	21:36

* Sunrise and sunset times have been calculated for the centre of Britain and Ireland (a point just south of the Isle of Man).

MAY'S MOON PHASES

1 MAY	◑	*Third Quarter*
8 MAY	●	*New Moon*
15 MAY	◐	*First Quarter*
23 MAY	○	*Full Moon*
30 MAY	◑	*Third Quarter*

NOTABLES

6–7TH The Eta Aquarids meteor shower can produce up to thirty meteors per hour. Coinciding with little moonlight means it should be unusually dramatic. The meteors are dust particles left behind by the comet Halley. Best seen after midnight.

9TH The planet Mercury is at its highest point above the horizon in the morning sky. Look for it in the east, just before sunrise.

23RD A full moon, known as the flower moon, may be seen in Britain and Ireland.

WILDLIFE

BIRDS

Tree pipits are in full song during May, choosing the tops of trees to trill and sing a descending scale, often flying into the air before 'parachuting' back to their favourite perch. Having migrated from regions south of the Sahara in Africa, the birds establish territories in broadleaved woodlands, clearings in conifer plantations and on isolated trees scattered across heathlands. They are more common in the north of Britain, having declined in southern England and Wales in recent years, and are infrequent in Ireland. Tree pipit nests are favoured hosts by cuckoos. The female removes one of the pipit eggs before laying her own. When this hatches, the cuckoo chick pushes the hosts' eggs or chicks out of the nest and the unsuspecting adult pipits end up rearing a cuckoo chick, which grows to more than double their size.

5th May is International Dawn Chorus Day. The early-rising species have evolved over time to make the most of the still morning air which helps their song carry further, while not eating into their foraging time as insects become active during the main part of the day. Why not head into a nearby park or wood at dawn to enjoy the audible wonder for your-self? There are even some mobile apps which use artificial intelligence (AI) to identify different bird species, and many work incredibly well.

INVERTEBRATES

In woodland clearings, especially near woodland ponds and wet ditches, keep an eye out for dragonflies and damselflies. Both hunt insects to feed on and are prehistoric in origin, found in fossil records. But can you tell the difference?

Dragonflies have two pairs of wings which are different sizes, the rear pair being broader and without a taper where they join the body. If you can hear it approaching, and it's flying strongly, often darting and making sudden changes of direction, it is a dragonfly!

Damselflies have wings which are the same size and shape. They are daintier, tend to stay nearer water bodies and you won't hear them flying.

There are eighteen species of resident dragonflies in Britain, and fourteen in Ireland. One of the most common seen in or near woodland, often patrolling or 'hawking' rides and glades, is the southern hawker, which is seen across most of Britain (but less widespread in Scotland). It is a fast-flying and agile species which hunts and catches its prey in mid-air. It has lime-green spots on a generally black body, with paler patches on its thorax.

MAMMALS

May is the end of the mating season for one of our most common woodland mammals, the badger, although implantation is cleverly delayed until the winter. Their young are born in February or March, and are often seen playing together above ground from May onwards. They live gregariously in a network of tunnels, known as a sett. Badgers feed mostly on earthworms, but also eat a varied diet of berries, nuts and even hedgehogs. They are habitual creatures, creating toilets to hold their pungent dung around the perimeter of a territory. They often run along well-known paths without much care and have been known to bump into unwary human visitors!

Bluebells (page 98) are still in flower across much of Britain and Ireland, reaching a peak in northern latitudes. Other flowers to spot include red campion and foxglove. The dainty flowers of wood anemone are in flower this month, most seen in the dappled shade of broadleaved ancient woodlands, and also thriving in coppice woodlands (page 29). Wood anemones are also known as the 'windflower' after a Greek legend. Beautiful young Adonis was fatally wounded while hunting wild boar in the forest. His mother Venus realised he was missing and searched for him in vain, finding only drops of blood on the forest floor. Venus sprinkled drops of nectar that she had brought to revive him. Where they fell, small white flowers appeared, stained with pink and purple from the blood of Adonis.

TRADITION AND FOLKLORE

The Celtic festival of Bealtaine (or Beltane) marked the first day of summer, which is now known as May Day. It has long been a moment to celebrate a new season and a coming time of plenty. Villagers elect a May queen and an accompanying Jack-in-the-Green (or Green Man), reflecting the importance of trees, then and now, in people's lives. Children dance around a maypole as part of the celebrations. It has always been considered a sign of fertility and, together with the merriment and cavorting around the village greens of England, attracted a ban from Oliver Cromwell and the Puritans. Maypoles were long lengths of any straight timber, harvested from a well-managed wood. At least one site in Britain is named after the tradition: Maypole Wood near St Helens.

Oak Apple Day takes place on 29th May to commemorate the restoration of Charles II to the throne after the English Civil Wars. In many parts of Britain, pageants have been traditionally held with revellers carrying sprigs of oak to mark the significance of the famous Royal Oak tree at Boscobel House in Shropshire. Charles II concealed himself inside the tree after Parliamentarian forces had defeated the royal army at the Battle of Worcester in 1651. It saved his life, and after surviving in exile for nine years, he reclaimed the throne in 1660.

Nicknamed the 'merry monarch', King Charles II restored festivities on May Day.

ARTS AND CRAFTS

ELDERFLOWER 'CHAMPAGNE'

From late May, the flowers of elder herald the coming of summer. Making the classic fizzy country drink of elderflower 'champagne' is surprisingly easy. This recipe relies on the natural yeasts present to create the fizz and alcohol. Just make sure you don't harvest too many flowers from a tree, allowing some heads to be pollinated so they can produce elderberries in the autumn, an important food source for many birds and mammals.

MAKES APPROX. 7L

Ingredients
10 elderflower heads
1kg white caster sugar
7l boiling water
3 lemons, roughly sliced
3 tbsp white wine vinegar

Materials: a square of muslin, and five–seven glass 1l bottles with sturdy swing-tops or plastic screw-top bottles. These must be sturdy enough to withstand the pressure from the developing fizziness. They must be sterilised.

Method
1. Pick the elderflower heads early in the morning so that natural yeasts are present. Choose a dry day to reduce likelihood of mould. Place the heads on kitchen paper for an hour or so to dislodge the many insects likely to be present (resist the urge to shake them off as you will lose much of the flavoursome pollen).
2. Dissolve the sugar in the boiling water and allow to cool.
3. When the water is lukewarm, add the elderflower heads (if too hot it will kill the natural yeasts). Add the lemon slices and white wine vinegar. Gently stir and cover loosely with a tea towel for twenty-four hours.
4. Strain through the muslin and decant into sterilised bottles.
5. Store the bottles in a cool and dark place. As the fermenta-

tion process is reliant on natural yeasts, the production of fizz is highly variable. Most of the fermentation takes place in the first seventy-two hours (putting the bottles in the fridge will halt the fermentation process). You might need to gently loosen the tops a little each day to release some of the pressure. Beware high pressure when opening!

6. Your elderflower 'champagne' should be ready to drink in about two weeks and could store for up to two months. Serve chilled, as for any classy bubbly. It makes a wonderful summer drink served with a variety of foods including smoked salmon, Swiss chard omelette and summer berry desserts.

TREE OF THE MONTH
HAWTHORN

White and odorous with blossom,
Framing the quiet fields,
And swaying flowers and grasses,
And the hum of bees.[20]

While ash, oak or Scots pine grab our attention with their impressive size and graceful features, hawthorn trees, despite only reaching 10m in height, are equally important for our identity and culture. They are the keystone species to our hedgerows, which stretch for more than 800,000km across Britain (more than to the Moon and back!), and 300,000km in Ireland. Hawthorn trees can survive for many hundreds of years, providing valuable habitat and food for wildlife. Their fruit, a haw, turns crimson red in autumn and persists on the tree through the winter. It is an important food source for birds in winter, second only to elder (page 56), and visited in particular by the fieldfare, redwing and waxwing, and our resident thrushes.

The prickly nature of hawthorn led to its widespread use for controlling grazing animals on farms, particularly when grown closely together and laid as a hedge with intertwined stems (see hedgelaying, page 14). Their thorns also protect small birds which choose to nest and roost within the safety of the tree's canopy. Modern hedges tend to be planted with a range of other species to add colour and diversity – like spindle, guelder rose, blackthorn, wayfarer and hazel – with hawthorn making up about two-thirds of the mix of a good hedge.

In Britain and Ireland, there are two species of hawthorn, the hawthorn and Midland hawthorn, but they commonly hybridise so telling them apart can be difficult. The Midland hawthorn is more common in the south of England where it fares better on heavier soils (e.g. clay); it is uncommon in Ireland. Generally, hawthorns are extremely resilient trees and can be found in some of the most extreme conditions on our hills and mountains, and along sea cliffs. It is often the only tree to survive in heavily grazed areas, saved only by its thorns. In these conditions, hawthorn provides a unique role in our ecology by being a founding tree, allowing more vulnerable thornless trees to grow under its protection. This means it helps natural succession of grassland to woodland, even with the appetite of browsing mammals like rabbits and deer, and domestic livestock.

The white and pink blossoms of hawthorn mark the arrival of spring, hence its other names: maythorn, or simply the may tree. Traditionally, hawthorn was considered a symbol of fertility and rebirth. Its blossoms were used for garlands and the soft green leafy branches of new growth used for outside decorations. However, there is a long-held belief that bringing hawthorn blossom indoors is unlucky, leading to illness or even death. In fact, hawthorn flowers contain an organic compound called trimethylamine which is released as a gas at room temperature and smells like decaying animal tissue, which may explain this association.

Knobbly stems and branches cut from hawthorn have long been used to make 'priests' and cudgels for fishermen and thieves alike. The timber of hawthorn is unusual in modern woodwork, yet its pinky hue and toughness lend it to a wide range of uses, including decorative inlays, engraving and small box-making. Traditionally, it was the wood of choice for mallet heads and the cogs of mill wheels.

The most famous hawthorn tree in Britain grows on a hill overlooking Glastonbury Tor. The original Holy Thorn of Glastonbury is reputed to have sprouted from the staff of Joseph of Arimathea, the man who buried the body of Jesus, although the current specimen is one of its descendants. In Ireland, where a solitary hawthorn grows in the middle of a field or clearing, it is known as a 'fairy tree', marking a gateway between the worlds of mortals and of fairy kind.

COLLECTIVE NOUNS

You could say that this almanac is a flight of yesterdays, a twinkling of todays and a promise of tomorrows. But what about collective nouns for trees and related subjects? Here's an intriguing list, part historical, part contemporary (also see page 230 for descriptive terms for groups of trees).

TREES AND FORESTS

A **blossom** of cherries
A **canvas** of maples
A **chamber** of boxes
A **ghost** of sycamores
A **grand democracy** of forest trees
A **joy** of almonds
A **majesty** of oaks
A **pack** of dogwoods
A **peel** of birches
A **shock** of cones
A **sledge** of acorns
A **throne** of ashes

A **tremble** of aspens
A **quiver** of yews
A **wisdom** of elderberries

FOREST WILDLIFE

An **asylum** of cuckoos
A **banditry** of tits
A **bevy** of roebucks
A **building** of rooks
A **cete** of badgers
A **charm** of finches
A **cloud** of butterflies
A **colony** of bats
A **crookedness** of crossbills
A **descent** of woodpeckers
A **dray** of squirrels
A **fall** of woodcocks
A **flight** of goshawks
A **glory** of bluebells
A **gushing** of galls
A **herd** of wrens
A **merl** of blackbirds
A **nye** of pheasants
A **parliament** of rooks
A **richness** of martens
A **scold** of jays
A **siege** of herons (in a heronry)
A **singular** of boars
A **skulk** of foxes
A **spiral** of treecreepers

A **swatting** of flycatchers
A **tiding** of magpies
A **train** of jackdaws
A **tok** of capercaillies
A **wisdom** of owls

PROFESSIONS

A **canopy** of arborists
A **grove** of foresters
A **kerf** of sawmillers
A **mess** of carvers
A **panel** of carpenters
A **tangle** of tree surgeons

CELTIC TREE ZODIAC

WILLOW

15TH APRIL–12TH MAY

You are the spirit of any place, graceful, lithe and ever youthful in body and mind. Highly sociable, you are quick to adapt to a situation and comfortable in the company of others. You have an innate ability to bind parts together, weaving strength and protection into every situation. When you choose to, you blossom like no other, attracting whispers of admiration from the wind. Compatible with Birch and Ivy.

HAWTHORN

13TH MAY–9TH JUNE

Whilst you may come across as a little prickly, you have a heart of gold. You are creative and extraordinarily resilient in the face of adversity. To the admiration of others, you are the first to spot opportunities to grow and prosper in almost any situation. Some say that you can be a little fey or overly romantic, but you are also very practical. Your willingness to lay yourself down and offer protection to others draws admiration. Compatible with Ash and Rowan.

JUNE

Beware the oak, it draws the stroke;
avoid the ash, it draws the flash;
but under the thorn; you'll come to no harm.[21]

THE MONTH AHEAD

This month we reach the longest day of the year, the summer solstice. In the garden and orchard, your hard work at other times of the year can allow you to sit back and enjoy the beauty of trees, with few tasks needed but much to see. An exception will be if you want to pickle some walnuts by following a simple recipe.

Birds, bats, flowers and more are all producing and nurturing their young this month, while a spotlight is shone on the graceful lime tree which is found in woodlands or parks, and is common along our streets. Keep a look out for extraordinary growths on their leaves – as though dozens of red nails have been hammered through each leaf – just one form of gall. The wonderful diversity of galls is celebrated, from oak apples to robin's pincushion.

If you come across some honeysuckle on a warm evening, take a moment to inhale its heady scent.

> *If Midsummer Day be ever so little rainy,*
> *the hazel and walnut will be scarce . . .*
> *but apples and plums will not be hurt.*[22]

DATES OF NOTE

3   June bank holiday *(ROI only)*
12 First day of Shavuot
16 Father's Day
17 Eid al-Adha
20 Summer solstice *(Midsummer's Day)*
22 Windrush Day

OTHER SPECIAL EVENTS

WORLD RAINFOREST DAY: an international day celebrating and promoting the importance of rainforests around the world, held during the third week of June.

PRACTICAL NOTES

IN THE GARDEN

June is a month to sit back and enjoy any trees and shrubs in your garden, with few tasks required during the month with the longest daylight hours. You could add some slow-release fertiliser to fruit trees, especially if you weren't able to provide them with a natural mulch earlier in the year.

Garden hedges might benefit from a trim, particularly evergreen species like box, privet and yew. Be careful to avoid disturbing nesting birds by observing any regular activities by parents arriving with food in their beaks or departing with the tell-tale pale faecal sacks of their young.

IN THE FIELD AND ORCHARD

Late June is the time of year to pickle walnuts if you are lucky to have access to some trees with fruit (technically known as drupes). Pickled walnuts are a curious English idea that raises eyebrows outside the country. Travel to famous walnut regions of the world, such as Grenoble in France, and you will find dozens of walnut products, including candied nuts, nougat and jam, tasty tarts and cakes, savoury breads, walnut oil and walnut-wrapped cheese. There will also be walnut drinks, such as aperitifs like eau de noix or ratafia, and even walnut wine. But nowhere will you find pickled walnuts!

Inspired by necessity, the English adapted to the effects of a climate which can result in under-developed nuts. Our summers do not always produce enough heat for some walnut trees to produce a good crop of fully formed walnuts (although, modern cultivars are much better adapted). Instead, the whole drupe can be picked before the shell has formed around the nut at its centre. The trick to test if you are on time is to push a strong needle into the centre. If you feel solid resistance, then the shell is forming and you are too late to pickle. To make your own pickled walnuts, you will find a recipe on page 149.

For apple, pear and other fruit trees, resist the temptation to allow all the young fruit to remain on the branches, as they will only sap energy from the tree. Thin out the smallest fruits by pinching them off, and the tree will put its energy into growing the ones left behind. Any branches struggling under the growing weight of fruit can be propped up with wooden battens or forked sticks (cut from any hedge laid during the winter).

IN THE FOREST

There is not much management required of trees this month, but any grass areas along paths and bridleways will need to be cut regularly before the sward becomes too long. Remember to leave as much uncut as possible to benefit wildflowers, invertebrates, amphibians and small mammals. Many managers cut rides on an alternate-year schedule, always allowing some areas to grow wild but not for long enough to allow the scrub to encroach. You, or volunteers, could record butterflies along rides and open glades. There are established recording methods provided by organisations who welcome data, while you will gain from understanding change over time in your woodland (another example of phenology). For the UK find out more at Butterfly Conservation (www.butterfly-conservation.org), and in Ireland visit the Irish Butterfly Monitoring Scheme (www.biodiversityireland.ie).

SUN AND MOON

SUNRISE AND SUNSET

DATE	SUNRISE	SUNSET
1 JUNE 2024, SATURDAY	4:52	21:39
2 JUNE 2024, SUNDAY	4:51	21:40
3 JUNE 2024, MONDAY	4:50	21:41
4 JUNE 2024, TUESDAY	4:50	21:42
5 JUNE 2024, WEDNESDAY	4:49	21:43
6 JUNE 2024, THURSDAY	4:48	21:44
7 JUNE 2024, FRIDAY	4:47	21:45
8 JUNE 2024, SATURDAY	4:47	21:46
9 JUNE 2024, SUNDAY	4:46	21:47
10 JUNE 2024, MONDAY	4:46	21:48
11 JUNE 2024, TUESDAY	4:46	21:49
12 JUNE 2024, WEDNESDAY	4:45	21:50
13 JUNE 2024, THURSDAY	4:45	21:50
14 JUNE 2024, FRIDAY	4:45	21:51
15 JUNE 2024, SATURDAY	4:45	21:51
16 JUNE 2024, SUNDAY	4:45	21:52
17 JUNE 2024, MONDAY	4:45	21:52
18 JUNE 2024, TUESDAY	4:45	21:53

19 JUNE 2024, WEDNESDAY	4:45	21:53
20 JUNE 2024, THURSDAY	4:45	21:54
21 JUNE 2024, FRIDAY	4:45	21:54
22 JUNE 2024, SATURDAY	4:45	21:54
23 JUNE 2024, SUNDAY	4:46	21:54
24 JUNE 2024, MONDAY	4:46	21:54
25 JUNE 2024, TUESDAY	4:46	21:54
26 JUNE 2024, WEDNESDAY	4:47	21:54
27 JUNE 2024, THURSDAY	4:47	21:54
28 JUNE 2024, FRIDAY	4:48	21:54
29 JUNE 2024, SATURDAY	4:49	21:54
30 JUNE 2024, SUNDAY	4:49	21:53

* Sunrise and sunset times have been calculated for the centre of Britain and Ireland (a point just south of the Isle of Man).

JUNE'S MOON PHASES

6 JUNE	●	*New Moon*
14 JUNE	◑	*First Quarter*
22 JUNE	○	*Full Moon*
28 JUNE	◐	*Third Quarter*

NOTABLES

20TH Summer solstice and the first day of summer.

22ND The full moon is known as the hay moon in Britain and Ireland.

WILDLIFE

BIRDS

Turtle doves are immortalised in the well-known carol 'The Twelve Days of Christmas' ('On the second day of Christmas, my true love gave to me, two turtle doves . . .'), the pair representing the Old and New Testaments. In fact, turtle doves are not present at Christmas time in Britain or Ireland as they spend the winter south of the Sahara in West Africa (in Senegal, for example) before arriving in June. They are one of our fastest declining birds, once common along woodland edges and hedgerows. Conservationists are encouraging landowners to sow more seed-producing ground plants and to allow them to regenerate naturally as the birds feed exclusively on the seeds of crops like wheat and oil seed rape, and wild plants such as chickweed, clover and plantain. The birds like to nest in dense and thorny trees and hedgerows (a similar habitat beloved by nightingales, page 94).

Birds of many species are fledging this month. In the garden, replace seeds and nuts at feeding stations with mealworms or fatballs. If you find a chick out of the nest and if it has feathers (i.e. a fledgling) leave it alone when it is not in danger. If it is featherless (i.e. a nestling) you should also try to leave it alone as its parents will continue to feed it, unless it is in danger from vehicles or cats (to name a few threats), in which case move it the shortest distance possible to a place of safety. You are probably being watched by its parents, so act quickly.

INVERTEBRATES

June is one of the best months of the year for butterflies, especially some common species such as the comma, small tortoiseshell and peacock, and those that migrate to Britain and Ireland, like painted lady. Those butterfly species which produce two broods a year, like the brimstone (page 72) and large white, are likely to be between broods, with the first not yet completing metamorphosis into adults so they are fewer in number. On a rainy summer's day, if you see a butterfly, it is likely to be the indomitable meadow brown. In woodland rides and clearings, look for the distinctive speckled wood.

MAMMALS

In our gardens, parks and woodlands, bats will be making the most of the rich harvest of flying invertebrates. The females will have given birth to a pup, and being a mammal, will be nursing them with milk. Young bats typically learn to fly in just three weeks but take a little longer to wean themselves completely from their mother and become effective hunters.

Keep an eye out for alexanders in the base of hedgerows which are reaching their full height of 1m or more. The plant looks like cow parsley but is thicker-stemmed and its leaves smell of celery. It can also be found near ruined farmsteads and castles because every part of this plant was once used, from the roots to the clusters of young cauliflower-like heads which were pickled.

Honeysuckle is in flower, livening up any walk along a hedgerow or woodland ride during the long evenings of June. Its heady scent provides one of the greatest pleasures for people visiting the outdoors in summer, while the flowers are an important source of nectar for many invertebrates.

The ingenuity of nature is full swing this month, with a whole range of cunning techniques being implemented by plants to help disperse their seeds. Sanicle (sometimes called ground elder) and burdock (as in dandelion and burdock) deploy hooks on their seed heads which catch in the coats of passing animals and clothes of people. These were the inspiration for the invention of Velcro.

TRADITION AND FOLKLORE

In Britain and Ireland, the summer solstice on 20th June is the longest day of the year. The Sun rises to the furthest north-east and sets to the most extreme north-west. At noon it reaches its highest point. It was a time of celebration for anyone connected to the land and food production, marking the start of the summer and an important time for ripening grain in the fields. Traditionally, a five-day pagan celebration followed Midsummer's Day, with bonfires, dancing and feasts held across Britain and Ireland.

If it rains on Midsummer's day, the filberts will be spoilt.[23]

Filberts are another name for hazelnuts (page 30), and the hazel tree has long been portrayed in myths and legends. The Celts believed that its nuts captured wisdom and inspired poetic creativity.

One legend tells of nine hazel trees which surrounded a sacred pool. In the autumn, their nuts would drop into the water to be consumed by salmon which absorbed the trees' wisdom. The number of bright spots on the flanks of a salmon are said to depict the number of nuts they have eaten.

ARTS AND CRAFTS

PICKLED WALNUTS

Pickled walnuts are a curious English delicacy. Rich in anti-oxidants, walnuts are an important part of a healthy diet. They are thought to help reduce inflammation in our arteries, lowering cholesterol and even reducing heart disease. Pickling them means that you can enjoy their benefits all year round, especially with cheese and cold meats.

Pickling walnuts takes about three weeks from picking to the end of the preserving process.

MAKES 3–5 228ML KILNER-STYLE JARS (JAM JARS)

Ingredients
1kg walnut drupes (freshly picked)

For the brine (you will need two batches)
1l water
120g table salt

For the pickling syrup
500ml malt vinegar
250g soft light brown sugar
½ tsp allspice
¼ tsp cinnamon
½ tsp whole cloves
½ tbsp fresh ginger, grated
1 garlic clove (optional)

Method

1. Pick the walnut drupes before the shell forms inside (see page 141 for details). You may want to check every walnut drupe with a strong needle, discarding those where you meet resistance from a hard shell inside.

2. Wearing rubber gloves (to avoid staining your hands) prick each walnut drupe with a fork a couple of times.

3. Combine the water and salt for the brine. In a bucket or other suitable container, add the walnut drupes and cover with the brine solution. Leave for one week.

4. Drain and repeat with a fresh brine solution (again, combining 1l water with 120g salt) and leave for another week.

5. Next, drain the walnut drupes and lay out in single layers on trays, in a dry and airy place. Within in a few days they will turn black (like your hands will still be if you didn't wear gloves!). You are now ready to begin the pickling.

6. Create the pickling syrup by combining all the ingredients in a large heavy-based saucepan. Bring the mixture to the boil.
7. Add the prepared walnut drupes and simmer for 15 minutes.
8. Remove from the heat and allow to cool slightly. Add the walnut drupes to sterilised jars, and when almost full, cover with the warm syrup mixture. Apply a tight-fitting lid.
9. Store the jars in a cool place, such as a garage or outhouse, and leave for at least one week to mature before consuming. They will last for at least one year.

TREE OF THE MONTH

LIME

A swarm of bees in June
Is worth a silver spoon.[24]

Britain has two species of lime trees, often known as the linden tree, and although neither are considered native in Ireland they are quite common. They are not related to the citrus fruit-producing lime tree which grows only in tropical conditions. Small-leaved and large-leaved lime also hybridise when they grow together, producing European or common lime which is a popular street tree. The little round seed heads of lime hang beneath a papery wing, dispersed by the wind when they spiral to the ground. In Britain and Ireland, our summers are not consistently warm enough for lime trees to produce viable seeds.

Lime trees are remarkably tolerant of difficult growing conditions, especially their legendary tolerance of urban pollution. Trees will resprout after cutting, even when cut down to the ground, and can be managed as coppice in the forest. Lime is rarely planted as a forest tree in Britain or Ireland, although it is often used by continental European foresters to help grow alongside high-quality oak. Instead, it is a popular tree in parks, woodland edges, specimen trees within hedgerows, and particularly for roadside avenues.

Lime trees are insect-pollinated, which is relatively uncommon among native tree species. They produce tiny pale green flowers in June or July, which are sweet smelling. Anyone standing underneath a lime tree could not mistake it for any other during the early summer as the whole tree literally hums with insects. In France, beekeepers are keen producers of lime honey (*miel de tilleul*), taking their hives to woodland glades and avenues of lime trees in early summer. The honey is very dark in colour and has a distinctive, slightly bitter taste. It is often found in French markets, and popular with home cooks, but is not so readily available in Britain or Ireland (though definitely worth searching for).

In summer, the lime aphid can feed in huge numbers on the underside of a tree's leaves. The pear-shaped insect only feeds on lime trees, the females having dark stripes along their backs. The aphids excrete large quantities of a dilute sugary solution while they feed, sometimes known as honeydew. Although it is sometimes collected by bees as a lazy substitute for nectar, it is otherwise a nuisance to people, causing surfaces of car windscreens, pavements and park benches to become unpleasantly sticky, and after rain, quite slippery.

The leaves of lime trees break down rapidly when they fall to the ground in autumn, fertilising the soil with nitrogen and phosphorous. In the garden, they are worth raking up and adding to a compost heap or used to make a rich leaf mulch.

Lime timber (known as basswood in America) is the most prized among wood carvers for its properties, used for centuries in intricate designs for church roofs and for the heads of rocking horses. It has long been the wood of choice for piano keys. One of the major by-products of lime was its bark which has remarkable strength (try snapping a twig to find out for yourself – the twig will break but the bark is almost impossible to tear apart). Lime bark, or bast, was once used to make baskets and in particular cordage and ropes but is now rarely used except among small-scale craft industries.

A warming climate is likely to benefit lime trees, helping them produce viable seed, and helping them spread further north into Scotland where their distribution is currently quite patchy.

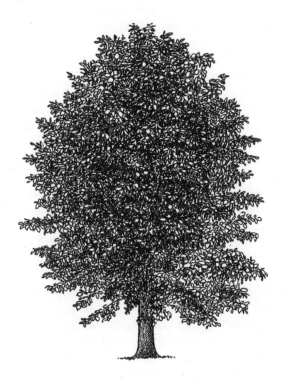

GALL STORIES

A gall is an abnormal growth produced by a plant under the influence of an invading organism, including fungi and invertebrates (for example, aphids, gall-wasps and mites). In the plant it results in an enlargement or a proliferation of cells, creating many weird and wonderful shapes. For the invading organism, the gall provides shelter and nutrients.

Oak Apple Day in the UK was celebrated at the end of last month. Despite its name, an oak apple is not a fruit because, of course, the fruit of an oak is an acorn not an apple. It is one of the many different types of gall that occur on dozens of different tree species. Some of the most well-known types of gall are oak apple and marble galls (oak), nail galls (lime), robin's pincushion (dog rose) and witches brooms (birch).

The oak apple gall-wasp (*Biorhiza pallida*) is a tiny invertebrate which lays its eggs inside the leaf bud of an oak. The galls appear on oak twigs between May and June. Inside each oak apple gall are several chambers, each housing a grub or larva. After going through metamorphosis, the young adults chew their way out of the gall and fly away, and so the cycle of life begins again.

Types of gall to spot on oak include:

- marble gall, once ground up to make very durable ink (used to sign the Magna Carta in 1215)
- knopper gall, which make acorns look like alien structures
- spangle gall, which grow on the underside of leaves
- artichoke gall, which turn oak buds into, you guessed it, artichoke-like structures

People who study galls are known as cecidologists. Why not enjoy a cecidological foray next time you walk past some trees? While most galls are prominent during spring and summer, others became easier to see later in the year when the leaves fall off the trees. Marble galls, for instance, turn brown in winter and remain on the bare twigs. Look closely and you will spot a tiny hole where the adult chewed its way out. If there is no hole, then the larva is still inside.

The British Plant Gall Society (which includes membership for people in Ireland) is a great place to find out more: www.britishplantgallsociety.org.

CELTIC TREE ZODIAC

HAWTHORN

13TH MAY–9TH JUNE

Whilst you may come across as a little prickly, you have a heart of gold. You are creative and extraordinarily resilient in the face of adversity. To the admiration of others, you are the first to spot opportunities to grow and prosper in almost any situation. Some say that you can be a little fey or overly romantic, but you are also very practical. Your willingness to lay yourself down and offer protection to others draws admiration. Compatible with Ash and Rowan.

OAK

10TH JUNE–7TH JULY

Strength is deep within your body and soul. Even when young, you possess a maturity beyond your years. Some may think you big-headed, but those who know you better can only watch in admiration at your incredible ability to foster and care for those around you. Even though you have a propensity to attract bolts out of the blue, your legendary strength means you are relied upon to build constructive and lasting legacies. Compatible with Ash and Reed.

JULY

St. Swithin's Day if thou doest rain,
for forty days it will remain;
St. Swithin's Day if thou be fair,
for forty days 'twill rain no more.[25]

THE MONTH AHEAD

Summer is in full flight. If you own any stone-fruit trees like cherry and plum, this is the time of year to get pruning. The same applies to walnut trees. Apple and pear trees need some tending this month too, and spare a thought for the Christmas tree grower who is already busy preparing trees for sale.

Walk through a woodland at dusk and you may be lucky to hear the classic 'hoooo-hu' of a tawny owl, or even the curious rasping calls of their young. Fruit is ripening in our woods, including bilberry and juniper 'berries'. Keep a good eye out for butterflies, whose numbers often peak this month.

Not every day in July is warm and sunny. Two fun tree-painting projects (page 172) might provide as much entertainment for adults as bored children on a rainy day.

Some sobering statistics reveal that though we may consider ourselves 'green' in Britain and Ireland, we have some of the fewest trees per person anywhere in the world, and it's not just our own health and wellbeing that is negatively affected. This month is a good time to plan any tree planting for the coming winter. If everyone planted one tree for every year of their lives, the world would be a better place and our souls enriched.

DATES OF NOTE

7 Muharram *(Islamic New Year)*
12 Battle of the Boyne *(bank holiday, Northern Ireland)*
15 St Swithin's Day
17 Ashura

OTHER SPECIAL EVENTS

NATIONAL MEADOWS DAY: held on the first Saturday in July, this day celebrates wildflower-rich grasslands across Britain, from large meadows to woodland glades.

NATIONAL DRAGONFLY WEEK: a week of activities in the UK for everyone to celebrate dragonflies, held in mid-July.

NATIONAL CHERRY DAY: a day in the UK to celebrate the beauty of the cherry trees, held on 16th July.

PRACTICAL NOTES

IN THE GARDEN

While St Swithin's Day (15th July) is a key day for weather watchers (the verse on page 159 explains why), traditionally it is also the best day of the year to prune walnut trees. Unlike most trees, which should be pruned when fully dormant during the winter months, walnuts should be pruned towards the end of the main growing season in mid-July. If pruned in winter they are likely to 'bleed' profusely, with copious amounts of sap flowing from any cut. As a minimum, this will weaken the tree; at worst it will increase the likelihood of infection by pathogens. Just remember that if it rains the same day, then we are likely to be in for a wet summer!

This is also the best time of year to prune stone-fruit trees such as cherry and plum. Most gardeners suggest you don't shred any prunings or add them to compost heaps as this can result in the spread of diseases.

Any trained apple and pear trees, such as a cordons, espaliers and fans, should be pruned now to keep them in good shape.

If you planted any large trees or shrubs earlier in the

year, keep a careful eye on them during any drought periods and be prepared to give each one a generous watering every day.

IN THE FIELD AND ORCHARD

Continue to remove small or under-developed fruit from your orchard trees. This not only helps the tree to invest more in the remaining fruit, it also helps prevent brown rot, caused by three species of fungi. Brown rot can be a serious problem if it strikes when the fruits of apple, cherry, pear and plum are beginning to ripen. Made worse by warm and humid days, it can be prevented by making sure that the canopies of fruit trees are not overcrowded. If you water the trees, keep any hose or sprinkler off the foliage and blossoms, instead watering the base of the tree.

Younger fruit trees will benefit from a summer cut. Older trees will not normally need to be cut if given a good winter prune earlier in the year, but if any branches become damaged by the weight of fruit or after a summer storm, remove them to help prevent further damage.

The same advice applies for certain species in the forest as it does to the garden or orchard. Whilst most foresters won't have plum trees under their care (though they may have cherry plum), they might have wild cherry and walnut (black or common) trees planted to produce valuable timber. Like their fruit-producing cousins (the same species but bred to produce fruit of a certain size or taste), cherry and walnut trees should be pruned this month and never during winter months.

Christmas tree growers will also want to shear their crop this month. A long-bladed shearing knife (a little like a bread-knife) is used to help improve the shape of the trees that are two–three years old, which also helps to stimulate new growth. The knife is wielded repeatedly like a machete, cutting from the top downwards to create the perfect triangular form.

JUL

SUN AND MOON

SUNRISE AND SUNSET

DATE	SUNRISE	SUNSET
1 JULY 2024, MONDAY	4:50	21:53
2 JULY 2024, TUESDAY	4:51	21:52
3 JULY 2024, WEDNESDAY	4:52	21:52
4 JULY 2024, THURSDAY	4:52	21:51
5 JULY 2024, FRIDAY	4:53	21:51
6 JULY 2024, SATURDAY	4:54	21:50
7 JULY 2024, SUNDAY	4:55	21:50
8 JULY 2024, MONDAY	4:56	21:49
9 JULY 2024, TUESDAY	4:58	21:48
10 JULY 2024, WEDNESDAY	4:59	21:47
11 JULY 2024, THURSDAY	5:00	21:46
12 JULY 2024, FRIDAY	5:01	21:45
13 JULY 2024, SATURDAY	5:02	21:44
14 JULY 2024, SUNDAY	5:04	21:43
15 JULY 2024, MONDAY	5:05	21:42
16 JULY 2024, TUESDAY	5:06	21:41
17 JULY 2024, WEDNESDAY	5:08	21:40
18 JULY 2024, THURSDAY	5:09	21:38

19 JULY 2024, FRIDAY	5:11	21:37
20 JULY 2024, SATURDAY	5:12	21:36
21 JULY 2024, SUNDAY	5:14	21:34
22 JULY 2024, MONDAY	5:15	21:33
23 JULY 2024, TUESDAY	5:17	21:31
24 JULY 2024, WEDNESDAY	5:18	21:30
25 JULY 2024, THURSDAY	5:20	21:28
26 JULY 2024, FRIDAY	5:21	21:27
27 JULY 2024, SATURDAY	5:23	21:25
28 JULY 2024, SUNDAY	5:25	21:24
29 JULY 2024, MONDAY	5:26	21:22
30 JULY 2024, TUESDAY	5:28	21:20
31 JULY 2024, WEDNESDAY	5:30	21:18

* Sunrise and sunset times have been calculated for the centre of Britain and Ireland (a point just south of the Isle of Man).

JULY'S MOON PHASES

5 JULY	●	*New Moon*
13 JULY	◑	*First Quarter*
21 JULY	○	*Full Moon*
28 JULY	◐	*Third Quarter*

NOTABLES

21ST The full moon is known as the grain moon in Britain and Ireland.

28–29TH The Delta Aquarids meteor shower peaks overnight although moonlight may hide all but the brightest. Best seen after midnight.

WILDLIFE

BIRDS

While swallows, swifts and house martins wheel across our blue summer skies, the cool and shady canopies of our trees and woodlands provide welcome shelter. Invertebrates emerge from every surface and direction, from the soil and under the bark, and along twigs and leaf margins, providing a feast for woodland birds and small mammals. The birds provide a great service to humans too, especially in our gardens and orchards where populations of unwelcome invertebrate pests are mostly kept at reasonable levels.

Our woodland specialist, the tawny owl, is busy feeding small mammals, especially voles, to its young who have now fledged but remain close to the nest. They still rely on their parents for food for about three months. If you walk at dusk through a parkland with old and hollow trees or through a broadleaved woodland, you might hear them begging for food. The young birds, still covered in downy plumage, make a rasping noise that sounds a little like someone sharpening a knife.

July is another great month to watch for butterflies and moths. The organisation Butterfly Conservation runs a simple garden monitoring scheme all year round (www.gardenbutterflysurvey.org), while the UK Butterfly Monitoring Scheme (UKBMS), which has been running since 1976, welcomes volunteers with time to commit to regular site visits for at least five consecutive years (www.ukbms.org). In Ireland, the Garden Butterfly Monitoring Scheme was launched in 2020 (https://biodiversityireland.ie/surveys/garden-butterfly-monitoring-scheme).

If you are out in the woods or walking anywhere through long grass or high heather during the summer months, be aware of the risk from ticks. These blood-sucking invertebrates prey on mammals, including domestic livestock, wild mammals, dogs and humans. At best, a tick bite can be painful and irritating. You should also be aware that ticks can carry a bacterium which causes Lyme disease. It can become a serious health issue but is difficult to diagnose. If you have been bitten, be vigilant if you experience headaches, fatigue, fever or a skin rash. If in doubt consult a medical professional. It is also worth visiting the website of Lyme Disease Action (www.lymediseaseaction.org.uk), which has useful information on reducing likelihood of a tick bite, how to remove a tick safely, as well as health symptoms and diagnosis.

Keep a look out for dragonflies and damselflies this month, with National Dragonfly Week in Britain taking place midmonth. Dragonflies are larger and stronger fliers than damselflies, which in contrast are daintier. Another difference is that dragonflies rest with their wings spread out from their bodies, whilst damselflies rest with their wings closed above their bodies. The azure damselfly is quite common in gardens, while the beautiful demoiselle might be seen near a woodland stream. Dragonflies can be seen near ponds and along woodland rides, especially brown and southern hawkers, emperor and common darter.

MAMMALS

You may immediately think of amphibians or fish in connection with ponds, but birds and mammals need water too and especially appreciate a source during prolonged dry spells. Even an old sink in a small garden can be turned into a wonderful mini-pond, and you might even catch an urban fox drinking from it at night. Remember to ensure that any thirsty mammal that might accidentally tumble in can get out again, by leaving a 'slipway' or steps made from stones, wood or even potted pond plants. Hedgehogs are particularly prone to drowning, as although good swimmers, they can become exhausted if they cannot climb out. Use the natural shade of a garden tree, even a dwarf variety in a pot, to help keep the water cool and prevent it evaporating too quickly. If you have a large pond, note that scientists have identified that the trees along ponds and waterways can reduce algal blooms, not just because of the shade they provide but also by the natural organic chemicals they release through roots and leaves.

PLANTS

In woodlands growing on acid soils (heather is a good indicator), this is the month that the tiny but delicious fruit of bilberry begins to ripe, traditionally picked from July through August. In Ireland, it is known as fraughan, from the Irish fraochán, where it is traditionally gathered on the last Sunday in July ('Fraughan Sunday'). It has different names across Britain, from whortleberry in south-west England to blaeberry in Scotland. It is common in most of the ancient Caledonian pinewoods of Scotland and an important source of food for wildlife. It's not uncommon to find fenceposts and rocks stained purple from the droppings of perching birds who have feasted on bilberry. Be warned, the berries will stain *your* hands and lips too!

Juniper, one of our three native conifer species, is in flower this month, its small yellow blooms followed soon after by juniper 'berries' (although technically they are cones). These are the key flavoursome ingredient for gin-making and have long been used as an accompaniment to game dishes.

TRADITION AND FOLKLORE

In Britain, St James's Day on 25th July was traditionally when Christian clergy visited orchards to bless the fruit. Trees were sprinkled with holy water and prayers recited by the assembled congregation. The ceremony was practised most in major apple-growing counties such as Gloucestershire, Herefordshire and Kent. In Sussex, young men would sound cow horns under the trees in a ceremony known as 'blowing the trees'.

The same day was also celebrated by hop growers, who cultivated this climbing plant which twines through small trees such as hazel.

> 'Til St James's Day is past and gone,
> there may be hops, or there may be none.[26]

ARTS AND CRAFTS

CHERRY TREE ART

Painting trees is fun at any time of year, especially on a rainy summer's day in July. Creating tree art is easy too, whether with the youngest of children or for your own enjoyment. Here are two techniques to try at home, drawing on the beauty of flowering cherry trees.

FINGER-PRINTED CHERRY

This a great way for a child to produce a beautiful and convincing tree. If you can't easily find twigs, you could use strips torn from a newspaper.

Materials and equipment: twigs of any size, paper, paintbrush, watercolour paints (tubes or solid blocks) in a variety of colours and glue

How to make

1. Collect a few twigs of different sizes from the garden, park or wood.
2. On a blank piece of paper (A4 is ideal but it could be any size), paint all over in blues or any other shade to create a simple background. For a sophisticated approach, older children could aim for a graduated look, with darker shades at the top and paler shades at the bottom.
3. Using the twigs, create a simple tree structure, using thicker twigs for the trunk and spindly ones for the branches. Fix them in place with dabs of glue once you are happy with the design.
4. When the glue is dry, use a range of reds, pinks and whites to paint the cherries all around the 'branches' – finger painting works brilliantly.

WIND-BLOWN CHERRY

This technique uses a straw to create 'blow art'. It is a particularly good activity with older children as it can produce very beautiful results, and although young children will certainly love having a go, be prepared for quite a messy result (and not just on the paper!).

Materials and equipment: paper, paintbrush, watercolour paints (tubes or solid blocks) in a variety of colours and drinking straws

How to make

1. Choosing a dark brown or black colour, add a couple of large drops of paint to the bottom corner of a piece of paper.

2. Using a straw, carefully blow the drops of paint up the page, following any 'branches' as they grow until they dry out. This is the main structure of your tree. Because you started in one corner and blew diagonally, your tree will be leaning, which naturally gives it a dynamic look.

3. Carefully add further drops of paint where you left off, this time using smaller drops of the same colour, and blow these in different directions to create more branches. Repeat until the tree's canopy is complete.

4. Alternating between red, white and pink colours, add a generous amount of paint to a large brush. Holding it about 20cm above the paper, tap the paint-laden brush gently against a finger on your other hand. Start cautiously, experimenting without over-wetting the brush (to avoid large splashes of paint). You are aiming to produce the illusion of cherry blossom in the tree's canopy.

5. For a more sophisticated result, you could use Indian ink for the tree which will repel watercolours when dry. This will allow you to easily paint a full colour background before adding the blossom. You could even try this technique with your homemade alder ink (page 77).

TREE OF THE MONTH
WALNUT

They planted me, a walnut-tree, by the road-side
to amuse passing boys, as a mark for their well-aimed stones.
All my twigs and flourishing shoots are broken,
hit as I am by showers of pebbles.
It is no advantage for trees to be fruitful;
I, indeed, bore fruit only for my own undoing[27]

Walnut trees are more common in Britain and Ireland than many people suppose. They can be found quietly masquerading as ash along hedges lining a country lane (they have similar compound leaves) and growing as self-seeded trees in glades and ride-side edges in our woodlands. Its dual utility as a high-value timber tree and a producer of nutritious nuts means walnut has suffered from some confusion among potential tree growers, perhaps unsure of which option to pursue. It can also be a little fickle to grow successfully and has some interesting impacts on neighbouring plants and animals (see below) where it grows in our parks, gardens and forests.

There are two main walnut species commonly found in Britain and Ireland. The common walnut (sometimes known as 'English') was introduced by the Romans, making it an honorary native tree in Britain. The earliest known planting of common walnut in Ireland was in County Waterford in the early 17th century. Its native range closely tracks the Silk Road, and it still grows in extensive forests in the mountains of Kyrgyzstan, Tajikistan and Uzbekistan. These are known as walnut-fruit forests because their understorey shelters apple, pear and plum trees, as these unique forests are also the origin of these important domesticated fruit trees. Black walnut is native to North America, especially the hardwood forests of the eastern United States of America, where it grows alongside hickory and tulip tree. The first record of black walnut growing in Britain is from 1656. Beyond these two species, there are some 50 species in the walnut family, which includes pecan and hickory.

Walnuts contain high levels of a phenolic compound called juglone. The trees exude it from their roots where it has the effect of reducing competition for resources from neighbouring plants. Gardeners soon discover that rhubarb cannot be grown near to a walnut tree, being highly sensitive to juglone. The natural compound is also found in its leaves and branches, and in summer heat it vaporises into the air to become a natural insect repellent. The large number of pubs called the 'Walnut Inn' or similar across England tend to be old coaching inns, named after the popularity of these trees planted to provide shelter to horses plus relief from biting insects.

The walnut is particularly choosy of its planting location, and it will reward the landowner who gives it the best quality fertile soil which is not prone to waterlogging. Famous herbalist John Gerard (1545–1612) captured this perfectly when he wrote that it prospered in 'fat and fruitful ground'. Walnuts are sensitive to late-spring frosts, so frost hollows should be avoided.

Along with wild cherry, walnut is one of the fastest maturing hardwood trees for foresters to consider when contemplating future timber markets. Both species produce marketable timber in about fifty-five years. This may sound like a long time to the lay person but compared to seventy years for ash or 120–150 years for oak, walnut is a 'fast-growing' productive hardwood tree. The timber of common and black walnut is often exquisite, having a rich honey tone and dark swirls in its figure, making it popular in furniture-making. Common walnut is the timber of choice for high-class gunstocks, having both beautiful figure and great elasticity, which is important for a rifle butt.

Both common and black walnut trees produce edible nuts, but in Britain and Ireland it is the common walnut that is more typically grown for this purpose. Many people believe that any walnut tree will produce nuts; while this is true in one sense, in reality there are some important differences between a randomly sowed or planted tree, and a deliberately cultivated walnut fruit tree. No one would plant an apple seed and expect it to grow into a specific variety like a Cox's Orange Pippin or Bramley. Just like the apple, there are many known varieties of walnut. These have been bred for their tree habit, nut flavour, size, ease of harvesting (e.g. shell thickness) and other parameters. Anyone serious about growing walnuts for their fruit should plant a grafted variety. The benefits are not only a nut of known quality, but they are prolific nut producers (a bucket of nuts is produced just three years after planting), whereas a typical seedling may take twenty years or more to produce a single fruit. Good walnut varieties for Britain or Ireland include Broadview, Franquette and Lara. Traditionally, it was believed that beating the tips off walnut branches helped to encourage more nut production (hence the quote above). This is not supported by modern pomology (science of fruit growing).

Walnuts can be harvested when the green husks of the drupes (a type of fruit) split open and release the nuts. Beware the black stains on your hand when removing husks as they are indelible! Some people like to pick walnut fruits before they mature to pickle them (page 149).

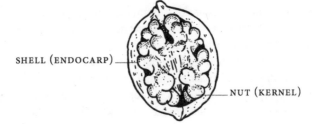

SHELL (ENDOCARP)

NUT (KERNEL)

TREES IN NUMBERS

FOREST AREA

There are 3.24 million hectares of forests covering the UK, representing 13 per cent of the total land area. The distribution of forest cover is quite unequal, with 46 per cent in Scotland, 10 per cent in Wales, 41 per cent in England and 4 per cent in Northern Ireland. The Republic of Ireland has less than 1 million hectares under trees (11 per cent forest cover).

Overall, Britain and Ireland are among the least-wooded regions in Europe. Denmark has 15 per cent, France 32 per cent, Austria 47 per cent and Finland 74 per cent forest cover.

About three-quarters of forest area in Britain and Ireland is privately owned. The proportion of conifers and broadleaves is roughly equal, whilst more broadleaved forest is owned by private owners.

TREE SPECIES

Sitka spruce is the most frequent conifer species in Britain and Ireland, after being introduced from the Pacific coastal forests of North America in 1831. These productive conifers cover more than three times the area than the next most frequent species, our native Scots pine.

Among broadleaves, birch is the most common species, followed by oak, ash, then sycamore.

TREES PER PERSON

People in the UK and Ireland live with the fewest number of trees per person anywhere in the world. Countries and trees per person:

- Canada 8,953
- Russia 4,461
- Australia 3,266
- Brazil 1,494
- United States 716
- France 182
- Ireland 154
- United Kingdom 47

What about the distribution of trees? Due to the inequality of distribution, on average most people in the UK have even fewer trees and woodlands, unless they live in rural Scotland and a small selection of other locations.

A total of 34 million people in the UK have poor to very poor levels of trees and woodland; less that 0.004 hectare of woodland per person, which means less than the canopy of one mature oak tree. A recent report from Friends of the Earth found that almost one half of all English neighbourhoods have less than 10 per cent tree cover.

Why does this matter? The lack of trees and woodlands

affects so many aspects of the natural environment as well as our own lives. There is good evidence that house prices in tree-less streets are lower than for identical houses in leafy streets. Lack of trees can lead to increased risks from seasonal flooding because trees growing in river catchments 'slow the flow'. We are missing out on benefits linked to health (e.g. reducing air pollution from traffic) and mental wellbeing (e.g. forest bathing). Benefits to society are among the many ways we gain from trees, known rather prosaically as 'ecosystem services' or more simply described as nature's benefits.

TAKE ACTION

Join a local community woodland. Groups are scattered across Britain and Ireland, and new volunteers are always welcomed.

Look out for local tree planting opportunities (or become a tree 'sapoteur'!).

Consider making a donation to a tree or forestry charity at home or abroad.

CELTIC TREE ZODIAC

OAK

10TH JUNE–7TH JULY

Strength is deep within your body and soul. Even when young, you possess a maturity beyond your years. Some may think you big-headed, but those who know you better can only watch in admiration at your incredible ability to foster and care for those around you. Even though you have a propensity to attract bolts out of the blue, your legendary strength means you are relied upon to build constructive and lasting legacies. Compatible with Ash and Reed.

HOLLY

8TH JULY–4TH AUGUST

Sometimes you hide in the shade of others, but everyone recognises your nobleness and tolerance. It is true that you can be a little prickly when young, but this is often a necessary trait to buck the trend and you soon grow out of it. In fact, your smooth features, together with the pure white soul you exhibit in later years, draws admiration at every turn. You are fiercely protective of those within your inner circle. Compatible with Ash and Elder.

AUGUST

August ripens, September gathers in,
August bears the burden, September the fruit.[28]

THE MONTH AHEAD

Fruit will be swelling and beginning to ripen in the garden, hedgerow and orchard, and young woodland birds and mammals tentatively beginning to explore the environment near their birthplaces.

August is a relatively quiet time for tree care unless a period of drought necessitates watering. Trees affected by drought may show visible signs, including leaf wilting or early leaf (or needle) fall.

This month will have a blue moon, which is a relatively rare event, occurring once every two or three years, hence the saying 'once in a blue moon'. Despite popular belief, this is not technically when two full moons occur in a single month, but when there are thirteen rather than the usual twelve full moons in a single year.

All wildlife may suffer at times of drought, so bear a thought for birds, mammals and invertebrates while you water your plants, and consider making a small watering hole or pond of any size in the garden. August is a good month for spotting some of our largest and most dramatic moths, like the poplar hawkmoth. Whisper a warning to them to watch out, it is also International Bat Night later in the month. You could follow the instructions on page 200 and make a bat box to boost numbers of these fabulous small mammals.

Britain and Ireland both have only three native conifers, one of which, the Scots pine, gains our attention this month, a tree which once provided masts for ships but now shelters precious wildlife.

DATES OF NOTE

1   August holiday *(Lúnasa) (ROI only)*
1   Lammas Day
5   August bank holiday *(ROI and Scotland)*
13 Tisha B'Av
26 Janmashtami
26 Summer/August bank holiday *(England, Wales and Northern Ireland)*

OTHER SPECIAL EVENTS

4TH Take part in a day of events to celebrate owls during International Owl Awareness Day.
24–25TH International Bat Night takes place on the last weekend of August.

PRACTICAL NOTES

IN THE GARDEN

If you have any large trees growing in a garden lawn, be bold and stop mowing regularly under the canopy. The longer grass will reduce evaporation from the soil and lead to less competition with the tree for nutrients and water. If you can live with this, next winter you could try adding some wildflower plugs and bulbs to the area and allow more wildlife into your garden. Not only that, but you will save yourself time and money by mowing less.

IN THE FIELD AND ORCHARD

While apple and pear trees require little work this month, some fruit trees will be ready to pick, especially cherries and plums. Plums are best picked before they become attractive to wasps. Some early varieties of apple may be ready towards the end of the month, and as these don't tend to store well, are best eaten fresh.

Try to delay cutting grass under your trees until any wildflowers have finished flowering and come to seed. This will ensure that the grassland continues to develop well and supports wildlife, especially insects, for years to come.

IN THE FOREST

August is a good month to plan future work because not much can be done in the forest. Hopefully you will have a management plan in place which will help you decide your long-term ambitions for the wood and how to achieve them. The plan should be compliant with national forestry standards, as this will help ensure your objectives are balanced between your own interests and the needs of the ecosystem. If you need help with this, professional agents can be hired, and grants may be available to assist you. Take a look at the myForest platform provided by Sylva Foundation, which helps managers map their woodlands and create management plans (www.myforest. sylva.org.uk).

SUN AND MOON

SUNRISE AND SUNSET

DATE	SUNRISE	SUNSET
1 AUGUST 2024, THURSDAY	5:31	21:17
2 AUGUST 2024, FRIDAY	5:33	21:15
3 AUGUST 2024, SATURDAY	5:35	21:13
4 AUGUST 2024, SUNDAY	5:36	21:11
5 AUGUST 2024, MONDAY	5:38	21:09
6 AUGUST 2024, TUESDAY	5:40	21:07
7 AUGUST 2024, WEDNESDAY	5:42	21:05
8 AUGUST 2024, THURSDAY	5:43	21:03
9 AUGUST 2024, FRIDAY	5:45	21:01
10 AUGUST 2024, SATURDAY	5:47	20:59
11 AUGUST 2024, SUNDAY	5:49	20:57
12 AUGUST 2024, MONDAY	5:50	20:55
13 AUGUST 2024, TUESDAY	5:52	20:53
14 AUGUST 2024, WEDNESDAY	5:54	20:51
15 AUGUST 2024, THURSDAY	5:56	20:48
16 AUGUST 2024, FRIDAY	5:58	20:46
17 AUGUST 2024, SATURDAY	5:59	20:44
18 AUGUST 2024, SUNDAY	6:01	20:42

19 AUGUST 2024, MONDAY	6:03	20:39
20 AUGUST 2024, TUESDAY	6:05	20:37
21 AUGUST 2024, WEDNESDAY	6:06	20:35
22 AUGUST 2024, THURSDAY	6:08	20:33
23 AUGUST 2024, FRIDAY	6:10	20:30
24 AUGUST 2024, SATURDAY	6:12	20:28
25 AUGUST 2024, SUNDAY	6:14	20:26
26 AUGUST 2024, MONDAY	6:15	20:23
27 AUGUST 2024, TUESDAY	6:17	20:21
28 AUGUST 2024, WEDNESDAY	6:19	20:19
29 AUGUST 2024, THURSDAY	6:21	20:16
30 AUGUST 2024, FRIDAY	6:22	20:14
31 AUGUST 2024, SATURDAY	6:24	20:11

* Sunrise and sunset times have been calculated for the centre of Britain and Ireland (a point just south of the Isle of Man).

AUGUST'S MOON PHASES

4 AUGUST	●	*New Moon*
12 AUGUST	◑	*First Quarter*
19 AUGUST	○	*Full Moon*
26 AUGUST	◐	*Third Quarter*

NOTABLES

12–13TH The Perseids meteor shower produces up to sixty meteors per hour at its peak and is one of the most dramatic of the year. Its bright meteors are fragments of dust left behind the comet Swift-Tuttle, discovered in 1862. Although the Moon may be quite bright, it sets after midnight, so early morning will be the best time to enjoy the show.

19TH The third full moon in a season with four full moons is known as a blue moon. Occurring every two and a half years, a blue moon is the thirteenth full moon in a single year and therefore falls outside the regular twelve named moons. Its rarity leads to the saying 'once in a blue moon'.

WILDLIFE

BIRDS

During the hottest times of the year, we are naturally drawn to water, and there is nothing better than a shady walk along a riverbank or canal towpath. Such places are also the perfect habitat for our most colourful of birds, the kingfisher. Its whistle often gives it away as it flies between perches, while the flash of orange and azure blue as it darts past is unmissable. They like to perch on branches overhanging still water where they can watch for their prey. They are particularly fond of minnows and sticklebacks, but will take fry (young fish) of any species as well as dragonfly nymphs, freshwater shrimps and tadpoles. Unlike a heron (page 298), they can't consume an adult frog. The riverside trees provide not only a perch for the hunter, but they also provide shelter for fry, especially among their roots where they extend from the riverbank. Alder and willow are especially important for fish stocks, and for conserving riverbanks during winter floods.

Take advantage of warm summer evenings and enjoy a late walk along a quiet country lane, park or woodland to listen out for owls. If you are lucky, you may catch sight of one, but you are more likely to hear one calling. Can you tell the difference?

Barn owls screech, and their eerie calls will send a tingle up your spine.

Tawny owls have several different calls but are instantly recognisable for their classic 'hoo, hu-hooo' call. Although widespread in Britain, they were absent in the wild in Ireland until first spotted in 2013.

The long-eared owl, which you are more likely to hear in a large coniferous forest, has a high-pitched call which sounds like a screeching gate.

The little owl can often be seen along hedgerows and woodland edges in Britain and has a low-pitched hoot and a 'chi'chi'chi' alarm call. It is very rare in Ireland.

Our fifth native owl, the short-eared owl, is not a woodland owl but can be seen hunting over rough pastures.

The warmer months of the year are the best for watching moths, with some of the largest and most spectacular appearing during July and August. One of our largest is the poplar hawkmoth, whose wings look like the dead grey-brown leaves of its namesake tree. However, when threatened it flashes a bright red patch on its underwing to deter predators. Its abdomen curves upwards and it rests with its wings outstretched.

The elephant hawkmoth loves to feed on the nectar of honeysuckle in a garden, park or along a forest ride, and is often most active at dusk. The pretty pink and olive-green bands of the adult moths make them difficult to miss. Their larvae (caterpillars) have distinctive large eyespots on their heads to deter predators.

In the UK, there is a National Moth Recording Scheme (NMRS) which has collected more than 30 million records submitted by volunteers. You don't need to be an expert or have a moth-trap to take part. Find out more at: www.mothrecording. org.

AUG

MAMMALS

International Bat Night is on 24–25th August (https://www.bats.org.uk/support-bats/international-bat-night). Why not join a local group for an evening walk, when expertise and equipment will be at hand to reveal the wonderful world of bats?

PLANTS

Wild carrot is in bloom, its delicate head of white flowers forming an upturned umbrella. Occasionally there is a single red flower at its centre, surrounded by white. It is also known as Queen Anne's lace on account of its dainty appearance, with the red splash of colour reflecting a drop of blood from the queen who pricked her finger while lacemaking. You may come across it in parks, field edges and hedgerows. Its root smells of carrot but is otherwise chewy and quite unpalatable, unlike modern cultivated varieties.

In Britain, the only native clematis, traveller's joy, can be seen rambling over hedge plants and woodland trees, its white flowers borne in clusters. It is also found in Ireland after being introduced more than one hundred years ago, where it is now considered a potential invasive species. The feathery seed heads gave rise to many other common names, such as old man's beard, hedge feathers and maiden's hair. Its thick woody stems were once smoked by country folk because they only smoulder when lit, lending themselves to another popular name, poor man's friend. The seedheads are popular with goldfinches in the autumn.

TRADITION AND FOLKLORE

Lammas Day (1st August) was first known as Lughnasadh by ancient Celts, honouring the Celtic god Lugh, and marked the 'festival of first fruits'. Indeed, the Irish word for August is Lúnasa, a variation of the spelling of Lughnasa. Starting on the eve of the night before, fires were lit to provide extra strength to the Sun whose powers were beginning to wane. A proportion of grain, fruit, nuts or livestock were burned as a sacrifice, thanking spirits for the harvest and beseeching them to be generous for the year to come. In modern Christianity, a freshly baked loaf from the new harvest is presented during the mass of the day.

You could bake some bread at home to mark the day. Incorporate herbs to bring a scent of summer to your baking, and rolled oats to mark the importance of grains on this special day.

ARTS AND CRAFTS

BAT BOX

This month is a good time to install a bat box so that it has weathered a little and can be explored by bats before they need to hibernate through the winter months. There are plenty of well-designed bat boxes available to purchase, though making your own is very satisfying, no more so when you watch the inhabitants emerging to feed at dusk.

This design is the Kent bat box, which is quite simple to make. Select untreated rough-sawn wood as this will provide grip for the bats. It may take several years for bats to find it but once installed you should leave it well alone as bats are protected by law and should only be disturbed or handled by those with an appropriate licence. Tell-tale signs of droppings and stains at the base of the box and on the ground are a give-away of habitation. On a warm summer's evening, you may even hear them chattering from inside.

Materials and equipment: rough-sawn wood (1800 x 300 x 20mm), a saw, 30mm screws and a screwdriver

How to make

1. The design has one long back-board, with two lengths in front of two differing lengths. Battens or strips of wood create crevices for the bats. These should be between 15–20mm and no more.

2. Cut the wood into the dimensions shown in the illustration, trying to keep edges square to limit gaps in corners (which the bats will dislike).

3. Add parallel and shallow saw groves on the surfaces below where the bats will land before entering the crevices.

4. Assemble the parts. You may need to drill small pilot holes to prevent splitting the wood, particularly in the battens and near any edges. You could nail parts together if you prefer.

5. Make sure the top edges are neatly aligned so there are no gaps under the roof when attached. The best way to achieve this is to cut through all five layers when assembled, pitching at a slight angle so that water will run off the roof.

6. Attach to a wall or tree so that the box is not too exposed to the sun during the day. Make sure you mount it beyond the reach of cats. Bats prefer a clear flight path too, so it should not be too crowded in by trees or fences.

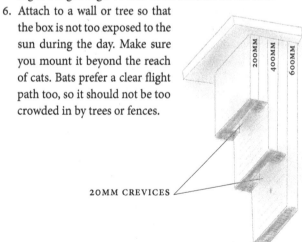

200MM 400MM 600MM

20MM CREVICES

TREE OF THE MONTH

SCOTS PINE

*Between every two pine trees there is a door leading
to a new way of life.*[29]

Scots pine is one of only three conifer trees native to Britain
and Ireland, the others being juniper and yew. After the ice
sheets retreated at the end of the last glaciation it was one
of the first trees to colonise much of the country. It came to
dominate much of the Highlands of Scotland but by the time
it was immortalised by Victorian tourists as an iconic symbol
of the 'wilderness' of the country, it was already vulnerable
and threatened. Its timber, being both lightweight and immensely strong, was much sought after for building, particularly for ships' masts. As a result of clearances for agriculture
and (ironically) the great afforestation efforts during the early
twentieth century, only some eighty natural areas of 'Caledonian pinewood' remain today.

Today, the value of Scots pine for tourism massively out-
weighs it timber value, while conservationists value its importance for many wild species of birds, mammals, plants, insects
and fungi. The Scottish wildcat, pine marten and red squirrel
rely on the tree to survive. The unusual crossbill, whose top

and bottom bills cross each other, has evolved over millennia to adapt perfectly to prising open pinecones to feed on the seeds within. Another unusual species, and Britain's heaviest ground-dwelling bird (it is extinct in Ireland), the capercaillie, roosts among the curving branches of old trees (often called 'granny' pines) and holds its breeding displays or leks in pine-wood clearings.

Scots pine is one of many different pine species, although many people tend to call any conifer a 'pine' tree. Close relatives are Corsican pine and European black pine. All three of these pines have needles that are bundled together in pairs of long needles. Other pine species have three, four or even five needles in a bundle, botanically called a fascicle. Although they are also conifer trees, those among the families of cedar, fir and spruce are not related and so should not be called 'pines'.

If you see a pine tree thriving on wet and boggy ground is unlikely to be a Scots pine but a lodgepole pine. This species was introduced from North America by foresters hoping to expand the country's forests into the uplands of Northern Ireland, Scotland and Wales in particular. Despite its economic origins, conservationists have been surprised to discover that some of the blanket plantations of lodgepole pine have become one of the last bastions of the red squirrel in Wales, which have adapted to feed on its seed. It has the benefit for red squirrels of seeding when quite a young tree so can quickly provide good habitat.

Scots pine timber is strong and lightweight, and although rarely used now for ships' masts, it's still used for telegraph poles. It is popular in joinery, such as for doors and windows, and is often called redwood or red deal by the trade. Pine leaves and resin contain terpenes, an important ingredient of turpentine, while the resin is hardened into blocks known as rosin and used by string musicians to add grip to their horsehair bows.

Pine nuts, much loved by pasta aficionados, often lightly toasted and sprinkled over dishes, or used as a key ingredient of pesto, are harvested from another species which grows in Mediterranean countries, the stone pine.

NATIVE TREES

Tree species that are native to Britain and Ireland are those which became naturalised without any help from us. There are about sixty species considered native in Britain and twenty-eight in Ireland, although conservationists and botanists are not always in full agreement. Compared to many other countries, we have a very limited number of native tree species, mostly because many species did not manage to return when the last ice age ended and before our landmasses were separated from the rest of the European continent. The count of trees native in France is about double Britain's, while in the USA, there are some nine hundred and fifty.

Among the sixty native tree species in Britain, only thirty-five are widespread. Most of these are broadleaved and only three are conifers: juniper, Scots pine and yew. What about the remaining twenty-five species? Most are very rare trees or sub-species, the classifications for which are often disputed, including seventeen micro-species of whitebeam (*Sorbus* spp.).

TREES NATIVE TO BRITAIN AND IRELAND

All the trees listed here are native to Britain and those with asterisks beside them are also native to Ireland. There are no species native to Ireland that are not also native in Britain.

COMMON NAME	LATIN NAME
Field maple	*Acer campestre*
Common alder*	*Alnus glutinosa*
Strawberry-tree*	*Arbutus unedo*
Dwarf birch	*Betula nana*
Silver birch*	*Betula pendula*
Downy birch*	*Betula pubescens*
Box	*Buxus sempervirens*
Hornbeam	*Carpinus betulus*
Dogwood	*Cornus sanguinea*
Hazel*	*Corylus avellana*
Midland hawthorn	*Crataegus laevigata*
Hawthorn*	*Crataegus monogyna*
Broom*	*Cytisus scoparius*
Sea buckthorn	*Elaeagnus rhamnoides*
Spindle*	*Euonymus europaeus*
Beech	*Fagus sylvatica*
Alder buckthorn*	*Frangula alnus*
Common ash*	*Fraxinus excelsior*
Holly*	*Ilex aquifolium*
Juniper*	*Juniperus communis*
Crab apple*	*Malus sylvestris*
Scots pine*	*Pinus sylvestris*
Black poplar	*Populus nigra subsp. betulifolia*
Aspen*	*Populus tremula*

Wild cherry*	*Prunus avium*
Bird cherry*	*Prunus padus*
Blackthorn*	*Prunus spinosa*
Plymouth pear	*Pryrus cordata*
Sessile oak*	*Quercus petraea*
Pedunculate oak*	*Quercus robur*
Purging buckthorn*	*Rhamnus cathartica*
White willow	*Salix alba*
Goat willow*	*Salix caprea*
Grey willow*	*Salix cinerea*
Crack willow*	*Salix fragilis*
Bay willow	*Salix petandra*
Purple osier	*Salix purpurea*
Almond willow	*Salix triandra*
Common osier	*Salix viminalis*
Elder*	*Sambucus nigra*
English whitebeam	*Sorbus anglica*
Common whitebeam*	*Sorbus aria*
Arran whitebeam	*Sorbus arranensis*
Rowan*	*Sorbus aucuparia*
Bristol whitebeam	*Sorbus bristoliensis*
Devon whitebeam	*Sorbus devoniensis*
Service-tree	*Sorbus domestica*
Round-leaved whitebeam	*Sorbus eminens*
Irish whitebeam*	*Sorbus hibernica*
Lancastrian whitebeam	*Sorbus lancastriensis*
Grey-leaved whitebeam	*Sorbus porrigentiformis*
Arran service-tree	*Sorbus pseudofennica*
Rock whitebeam	*Sorbus rupicola*
Somerset whitebeam	*Sorbus subcuneata*
Wild service-tree	*Sorbus torminalis*
Bloody whitebeam	*Sorbus vexans*

Wilmott's whitebeam	*Sorbus wilmottiana*
Yew*	*Taxus baccata*
Small-leaved lime	*Tilia cordata*
Large-leaved lime	*Tilia platyphyllos*
Gorse*	*Ulex europeaeus*
Wych elm*	*Ulmus glabra*
Field elm	*Ulmus minor*
Guelder rose*	*Viburnum opulus*

CELTIC TREE ZODIAC

HOLLY

8TH JULY–4TH AUGUST

Sometimes you hide in the shade of others, but everyone recognises your nobleness and tolerance. It is true that you can be a little prickly when young, but this is often a necessary trait to buck the trend and you soon grow out of it. In fact, your smooth features, together with the pure white soul you exhibit in later years, draws admiration at every turn. You are fiercely protective of those within your inner circle. Compatible with Ash and Elder.

HAZEL

5TH AUGUST–1ST SEPTEMBER

Otherworldly and irrepressible in equal measure, you possess a unique ability to regenerate. Always positive and energetic, you bend and pleach to support others, whatever their burden. Your generosity regularly involves nurturing those around you, plying them with a harvest of goodness, however tiny and precious. While everyone recognises your fierce intelligence, some believe you have magical powers to bewitch and enthral the supernatural. Compatible with Hawthorn and Rowan.

SEPTEMBER

September blow soft
'til the fruit's in the loft.[30]

THE MONTH AHEAD

In folklore, if a 'worm' (insect larva) is found inside a gall (page 155) on Michaelmas Day (29th September), then the year will bring good fortune, but if a spider is inside, then it will be a bad year with food shortages and ruined crops. Michaelmas comes near the autumn equinox, marking the end of summer and the beginning of autumn.

Fruit trees are laden with ripening fruit and anyone with a garden or orchard will soon be very busy picking it. In fact, the full moon this month is known as the fruit moon. On the same night, a partial lunar eclipse will be visible from anywhere in Britain or Ireland (cloud-allowing!). There are wild fruits galore in the countryside as well, and who can refuse the plump black-purple of a ripe bramble fruit or blackberry!

Wood ants are amazing creatures and their impressive mounds in a sunny woodland clearing are worth seeking out. If you spot a grey squirrel in your local park or in a forest, question your feelings for the creature, which as a fault not of its own making, has become a serious pest in Britain, which threatens the existence of our native red squirrel.

DATES OF NOTE

7   Ganesh Chaturthi
14 Holy Rood *(Nutting Day)*
16 Milad un Nabi *(Mawlid)*
22 Autumn equinox
29 Michaelmas *(All Angels)*

OTHER SPECIAL EVENTS

In the UK, September is NATIONAL ORGANIC MONTH.

21–22ND EUROPEAN HERITAGE DAY IN ROI.

SEP

PRACTICAL NOTES

IN THE GARDEN

This is a good time to plant spring-flowering bulbs, like crocuses and daffodils, around the base of any trees in your garden.

Make sure your compost bin or heap is ready to receive an influx of tree leaves next month.

If you have room for any new trees or shrubs in the garden, now is a good time to decide what to plant and place an order. A good-quality tree nursery will not deliver until the trees are fully dormant in winter, while ordering early means you are more likely to receive your choice of species or variety.

IN THE FIELD AND ORCHARD

Apples will be ripening on trees this month. When ripe they will easily come away from the branch given a gentle tug. If they come away with part of the branch, then they are not ripe (and you pulled too hard)! Those ripe now are still relatively early fruiters so are best eaten fresh. The general rule is that the later the ripening, the better the storing qualities. To store apples for the winter, carefully wrap each fruit in a single sheet of newspaper and arrange them in single layers on a tray or shelf.

If you have any plums left on a tree, then pick them now before they spoil. They can be frozen too; remove their stones and open freeze in a single layer before bagging up into handy batches for winter pies and crumbles.

Landowners can also consider agroforestry as an approach to combining food production with timber production. In theory, adding trees to a farming system can improve biodiversity and even food productivity, while growing food under trees can help tackle the challenging economics of growing trees. In practice, getting the balance right can be difficult to achieve but there are many innovative examples of silvo-arable (e.g. trees and wheat or barley), silvo-pastoral (e.g. trees and sheep), and even silvo-poultry (e.g. trees and egg production or broilers). Such approaches may also help create systems that are more resilient in the face of climate change. Many of these systems are also run under organic conditions.

IN THE FOREST

September is the start of the busy woodland management season. As the leaves fall and wildlife has settled after the breeding season, tree felling can soon begin. Make sure you comply with relevant laws, which dictate what and how much is permissible to fell without permission. You can mark trees you want to fell or retain using florescent paint applied to their stems. Some experienced foresters will do this by eye, while there are more formal approaches which take a mathematical approach. Forestry is often described as both a science and an art. Considering the long timescales and the implications of any errors in planning and practice, this description is very apt.

SUN AND MOON

SUNRISE AND SUNSET

DATE	SUNRISE	SUNSET
1 SEPTEMBER 2024, SUNDAY	6:26	20:09
2 SEPTEMBER 2024, MONDAY	6:28	20:07
3 SEPTEMBER 2024, TUESDAY	6:30	20:04
4 SEPTEMBER 2024, WEDNESDAY	6:31	20:02
5 SEPTEMBER 2024, THURSDAY	6:33	19:59
6 SEPTEMBER 2024, FRIDAY	6:35	19:57
7 SEPTEMBER 2024, SATURDAY	6:37	19:54
8 SEPTEMBER 2024, SUNDAY	6:39	19:52
9 SEPTEMBER 2024, MONDAY	6:40	19:49
10 SEPTEMBER 2024, TUESDAY	6:42	19:47
11 SEPTEMBER 2024, WEDNESDAY	6:44	19:44
12 SEPTEMBER 2024, THURSDAY	6:46	19:42
13 SEPTEMBER 2024, FRIDAY	6:47	19:40
14 SEPTEMBER 2024, SATURDAY	6:49	19:37
15 SEPTEMBER 2024, SUNDAY	6:51	19:35
16 SEPTEMBER 2024, MONDAY	6:53	19:32
17 SEPTEMBER 2024, TUESDAY	6:55	19:30
18 SEPTEMBER 2024, WEDNESDAY	6:56	19:27

SEP

19 SEPTEMBER 2024, THURSDAY	6:58	19:25
20 SEPTEMBER 2024, FRIDAY	7:00	19:22
21 SEPTEMBER 2024, SATURDAY	7:02	19:20
22 SEPTEMBER 2024, SUNDAY	7:03	19:17
23 SEPTEMBER 2024, MONDAY	7:05	19:15
24 SEPTEMBER 2024, TUESDAY	7:07	19:12
25 SEPTEMBER 2024, WEDNESDAY	7:09	19:10
26 SEPTEMBER 2024, THURSDAY	7:11	19:07
27 SEPTEMBER 2024, FRIDAY	7:12	19:05
28 SEPTEMBER 2024, SATURDAY	7:14	19:02
29 SEPTEMBER 2024, SUNDAY	7:16	19:00
30 SEPTEMBER 2024, MONDAY	7:18	18:57

* Sunrise and sunset times have been calculated for the centre of Britain and Ireland (a point just south of the Isle of Man).

SEPTEMBER'S MOON PHASES

3 SEPTEMBER	●	*New Moon*
11 SEPTEMBER	◑	*First Quarter*
18 SEPTEMBER	○	*Full Moon*
24 SEPTEMBER	◐	*Third Moon*

NOTABLES

18TH A full moon, known as the fruit moon in Britain and Ireland. It is also a super full moon as it is closest to Earth in its orbit, making it appear larger and brighter than usual.

18TH A partial lunar eclipse will be visible as the Moon passes through the Earth's partial shadow (penumbra) and part of its darkest shadow (umbra).

22ND Autumn equinox falls when the length of day and night is exactly equal. This marks the first day of autumn.

WILDLIFE

BIRDS

As the juicy larvae of butterflies and moths dwindle, many birds switch their diet to the new harvest of fruits, nuts and seeds produced by plants. The fruit of blackthorn (sloe), elder (berry), hawthorn (haw) and dog rose (hip) ripen to provide important reserve-building nutrients for birds. Take a pair of binoculars with you as you walk in the park, along a hedge-row or in the woods to watch blackbirds and song thrushes feeding.

INVERTEBRATES

Coming across the shifting surface of a wood ant nest in a forest is a thrilling experience. There are three different species of wood ant, all of which build mounded nests above ground. The hairy wood ant is found in Scotland and through north-ern England into mid-Wales, where it prefers quite sunny sites so is usually found in young woodlands where the canopy is less dense or along woodland edges. The Scottish ant, as its name suggests is found in Scotland, where it is more tolerant of shade and therefore found in more mature pinewoods. It is also the only species present in Ireland that builds mounded nests. The southern wood ant is our largest species (workers are 10mm and queens are 12mm) and is found across southern Britain, preferring sunny locations in conifer forests. Never poke a nest with a stick. Instead sit quietly nearby and watch the mesmerising activities of the ants guarding the nest and carrying materials to and fro.

MAMMALS

Grey squirrels appear to be very active this month as they hunt for seeds and nuts in the trees. Many people love to watch their high jinks and their cute appearance, and they have become a familiar species, particularly in our towns and cities where they are confident around people. Sadly, this species has become a significant pest since it was introduced to Britain from North America in 1876, and to Ireland in 1911. Foresters must control numbers to reduce the impact the grey squirrel has on trees, where its bark-stripping antics cause trees to partially lose their canopy (effectively being ring-barked), leaving them vulnerable to snapping by the wind and attacked by pathogens; while damaged trees lose all timber value. Tragically, it has also had a disastrous impact on our native red squirrel; being a larger and more aggressive species, the grey squirrel has pushed the red into smaller and smaller areas. Even more critically, the grey squirrel carries a pox which it is resistant to, but which is always fatal to a red squirrel. Scientists are working on a contraceptive to control grey squirrel numbers, while conservationists are hoping that the recent reintroduction of pine martens, which are a lethal predator, will eventually help reduce populations of this troublesome pest. Red squirrels, being more agile and lighter, can retreat to branch tips to avoid a hunting pine marten.

PLANTS

The pretty pink flowers of herb robert are quite common in shady places under trees and hedgerows, while in the garden it is often considered a weed. Each flower has five petals with round tips, held aloft on red-green stems whose smell is quite unpleasant (another colloquial name is stinking robert). The plant was associated with the goblin (sometimes fairy or sprite) known as Puck or Robin Goodfellow, who would complete helpful domestic chores around the house but was just as likely to be a great mischief, his pranks undoing any good.

The juicy fruits of bramble ripen this month, challenging anyone who may have cursed its prickles at every other time of the year. Going blackberrying is one of the few foraging behaviours that has survived to modern times. Whether you love to eat freshly picked fruit or make homemade jam or pies, just remember to avoid picking low down in the dog leg-cocking zone or along busy roads where the fruits will have absorbed all sorts of nasty chemicals, including heavy metals.

FUNGI

Dense clusters of sulphur tuft can often be seen this month growing from rotting stumps and logs in both broadleaved and coniferous woodlands. Their caps are the colour of sulphur, while the gills are a purple-black colour. It smells strongly of mushrooms but it is not edible.

TRADITION AND FOLKLORE

NUTTING DAY

*This day they say, is nutting day
and all the youths are now a-nutting gone.*[31]

Holy Rood or Holy Cross Day on 14th September is also known as Nutting Day. In a centuries-long tradition, it was the youth especially who collected hazelnuts on this feast day. The phrase 'going a nutting' soon became associated with seduction, sex and, inevitably, the devil himself. With the young cavorting in the woods alone, perhaps it is no surprise that sayings like this found their way into our folklore: 'A good year for nuts, a good year for babies.'

Collecting nuts on other days in September was to be avoided, and only the brave or foolish would do so on a Devil's Nutting Day (21st September). In Sussex, there is a long-held superstition that gathering nuts on a Sunday was to be avoided as the devil himself will be nutting in the woods, especially after sunset when it was 'as black as the devil's nutting bag.'

ARTS AND CRAFTS

AUTUMN LEAVES PRESERVATION

Have you ever found the perfect autumn leaf, bright with flames of red, orange and yellow, and wished that you could preserve it? Look no further. Here's an easy and fun way to preserve autumn leaves that can be used to decorate the home or office, create bookmarks, mount in a clip frame, punch a hole through and hang from a string mobile, and countless other creative uses. This is a great activity with children, just make sure you supervise the use of the hot iron.

Materials and equipment: waxed paper sheets (not greaseproof paper) or waxed bags, electric iron and scissors

How to make
1. Collect leaves from your favourite trees in the park, forest or garden.
2. Prepare them for preserving. Make sure they are dry, then trim any stalks you don't want to keep and separate any overlapping leaves if you want to encapsulate a whole sprig.
3. Lay out two sheets of waxed paper, making sure the waxed

surfaces face inwards (otherwise it will make a mess of the iron and the surface below!). If you can get hold of waxed bags, then this is even easier.

4. Lay out the leaves on one of the waxed sheets, ensuring they don't overlap one another. Lay the other waxed sheet on top – you should now have a sandwich-filling of leaves laid out between the two sheets of waxed paper.

5. With the iron heated to a low setting, work across the top sheet. Press gently and work in one direction to avoid air bubbles. With thicker leaves you may need to linger longer. The aim is to heat the paper over each leaf just enough to melt the wax. The paper will change from translucent to transparent. With thicker leaves, you may need to also iron the reverse side. Allow the wax to cool and harden before handling further.

6. Cut carefully around the waxed leaves with scissors. Get creative!

TREE OF THE MONTH

OAK

If acorns abound in September,
snow will lie deep in December.[32]

The English have made it a habit to name trees after themselves, the oak being just one of many. In fact, there are two oak species native to Britain and Ireland, neither of which is any more English than it is Irish, Scottish or Welsh. The pedunculate oak and sessile oak are certainly iconic trees to people in Britain and Ireland and deeply engrained in culture, being the main timber for construction for houses, machinery, and of course shipbuilding. Around the world there are some six hundred species of oak, but most of these will not be found commonly growing in Britain or Ireland.

Specimens of oak (both species) are among our oldest trees, some dating to more than a thousand years old, and there are at least seven hundred individually named trees across Britain and Ireland. Most well-known of all in Britain is the Major Oak in Sherwood Forest, of Robin Hood fame, while the Belvoir Oak in Belfast is estimated to be at least five hundred years old. The King Oak near Tullamore in Ireland might be as old as eight hundred years.

The pedunculate and sessile oak species can often be identified quite easily, although they also hybridise, in which case they exhibit a blend of characteristics making it more difficult. Pedunculate oak is named after the short stalk or 'peduncle' from which the acorn grows away from the stem. The acorns of sessile oak grow without a stalk ('sessile' meaning fixed or immobile). There are also differences in the leaves, with those of pedunculate having little lobes at their base, whereas leaves of sessile oak stretch forward away from the leaf stalk.

Both species of native oak grow across the whole of Britain and Ireland, although sessile oak is more common in the west of both islands. It is especially associated with the temperate rainforests of south-west England, Wales, north-west Britain, Scotland and some parts of Ireland (such as the Vale of Clara). These special habitats are unique anywhere in the world, and just as important for wildlife as the more famous tropical rainforests. The typically wet and humid conditions favour lichens, mosses and ferns, which cloak the surfaces of rocks and trees in luxuriant green.

Oak trees were traditionally the main crop for foresters producing timber for industry. In areas of England like the New Forest and Forest of Dean, where the trees lay close to navigable waters, there were even laws restricting any oak trees felled to be used for shipbuilding. Foresters would make sure that certain trees grew in ways which naturally created the bent timber needed for ships' knees, or straight and true for planking. Oak trees were also commonly grown in mixtures with coppice hazel (page 29), creating the tall standard trees on long rotations (one hundred and twenty–one hundred and fifty years to produce timber) with the hazel coppiced on five–eight-year cycles.

Any carpenter who works with oak will know that if they leave a tool resting on the timber it will soon stain. The high tannin content in oak is corrosive to iron and mild steel. The high tannin content in oak has long been exploited. Oak bark was once the material of choice for tanning leather. Barrels for alcohol production are still made from oak, as they have been for centuries, with the natural tannins present in the wood being an important part of flavour and character development during maturation. Most whisky is produced in barrels which have been 'seasoned' first to make sherry or bourbon.

The natural phenology of oaks is interesting to observe and has long-been a curiosity for country people, hence sayings such as 'Oak before ash, then only a splash' (page 85). The warmer the conditions in spring, the earlier that oak will flush before ash. Many people will overlook the tiny green goblet-shaped female flowers produced on new growth each spring, noticing instead the more obvious dangling green male catkins which grow from the previous year's twigs. Oak has a second burst of growth in late summer, called 'lammas growth' because it starts around Lammas Day on 1st August when the grain harvest was traditionally celebrated.

The quantity of acorns produced by oak trees in autumn tend to vary every three–four years, peaking during 'mast years'. Traditionally, autumn was an important time of year for herders to fatten their pigs, with acorns being a favourite and potent form of protein. The common right to access forests for this reason is known as 'pannage' and is enshrined in law which dates to the time of William the Conqueror.

Oak remains one of the most important timbers for renovating ancient timber-framed buildings, constructing sustainable new buildings, outdoor furniture and more. It is highly durable, meaning that it lasts well outdoors, even when exposed to the weather and even in waterlogged soils. In furniture-making, it is highly prized for its strength and appearance. A particular way of cutting an oak log, known as a 'quarter sawing', exposes the medullary rays within the timber which adds attractive character to its figure.

COPSE, WOOD OR FOREST

When is a forest not a Forest, and a wood not a copse, but a spinney? Here is a list of descriptive terms for groups of trees, from arboretum to xylarium.

Arboretum (plural **arboreta**): botanical collection of trees, often supporting public education and science activities, including genetic conservation.

Avenue: a row of trees, often a double row, marking an approach to a feature or lining the sides of a road, e.g. lime avenue.

Beare: an old Anglo-Saxon term for a small wood.

Brake: a thicket, typically of shrubs.

Bush: wooded area but usually not densely populated with trees.

Cant: block within a woodland (usually one–two hectares) often used to describe an area under coppice management, with the number of cants equal to the rotation length (e.g. with fourteen-year coppice rotation, there will be fourteen cants).

Carr: a wet woodland, typically of trees which like these conditions, especially alder and willows.

Chaparral: dense thickets of trees in the Mediterranean region of Europe, California and Mexico, usually comprising evergreen broadleaved species adapted to hot, dry summers.

Clearing: an area clear of trees in a wood or forest, sometimes created when trees are felled for timber or kept free to enhance biodiversity or landscape.

Clump: hilltop group of trees, often prominent in the landscape.

Coed: Welsh name for forest.

Coille: Gaelic name for forest, commonly used to name sites in Ireland and Scotland.

Compartment: the management unit of a forest, used as a technical term among foresters to define areas under similar management or with discrete mixtures of tree species.

Coppice: the management practice of coppicing, although sometimes used to describe an area managed as a coppice crop, e.g. sweet chestnut coppice.

Copse: technically an area managed as coppice but commonly used to describe a small wood.

Coupe: an area within a woodland where the trees are to be felled.

Dell: small valley or hollow, usually (but not always) covered with trees.

Dingle: commonly used in Wales to describe a steep-sided wooded valley.

Forest or forest: with a capital 'F', it refers historically to a royal hunting forest (e.g. the Forest of Dean, the New Forest), but in modern usage, with a lowercase used widely, it describes a large area of trees, often used interchangeably with wood or woodland.

Grove: a small group of trees, generally of an attractive nature.

Hagg: a clearing in a wood or forest, from Old Norse, and used still in northern England.

Hanger: a small group of trees on a hillside or slope.

Hedge or hedgerow: a line of trees, often comprising shrub species, traditionally planted and maintained to mark a boundary or to contain livestock. In some parts of England, such as Devon, they are planted on top of soil-filled double stone walls. Traditionally managed by laying, and sometimes with occasional large trees left uncut to grow as 'standards'.

Holt: a wooded hill.

Krummholz: trees growing at high latitudes and in exposed situations where their growth is stunted by extreme cold and wind, creating dwarfed and contorted forms.

Monoculture: a group of trees consisting of a single species (e.g. in a plantation) or genetic similarity (e.g. a natural group of clonal aspen grown from suckers).

Orchard: an area of trees planted and managed for their crop of fruit or nuts, typically using specific varieties to improve food quality and volume production.

Pinetum: a collection of pine (*Pinus* spp.) trees, or more often conifers generally, forming a special type of arboretum.

Plantation: an area of trees deliberately planted as a forest operation, typically for timber production although not exclusively.

Quercetum: a collection of oak (*Quercus* spp.) trees forming a special type of arboretum.

Roundel: a small group of trees circular in shape (cf. clump).

Shelterbelt: a band of trees planted or managed to protect soil, crops and livestock from damaging winds.

Shrubbery: an area of small trees (shrubs) in a garden.

Spinney: a small area of trees, like a copse or wood but traditionally created and managed for hunting game.

Stand: a forestry term used to describe an area of a forest with uniform tree species, structure, age and size, etc., similar to a compartment.

Thicket: a dense area of trees, often impenetrable to people.

Withy: a group of willows, often in a damp or boggy area.

Wood; or woodland: both terms are used interchangeably, see also forest.

Xylarium: a collection of woody specimens, as a 'herbarium' is for plants.

ALL A SPINNEY

Hunting for game, so I thought
in the spinney, not for trees,
but soon so fiercely distracted
by leaf, bole and canopy.

Traversing hot chaparral,
crawling under krummholz,
fighting through beare and thicket,
eye fixed upon distant clump and hanger.

A passage framed with silver lime
along a double avenue, past an orchard,
before the thickening bush and lively copse
of wood and forest.

The workers watched and toiled,
while the coppice stood
over by giant standards,
hemmed in by hedge and row.

When from a clearing,
beyond the coupe and shrubbery,
I spied her shimmering samara,
beckoning me through the cant.

She sat proud, amidst the holt
of the rising roundel above the dell,
though others had fared less well
in the hagg or withy.

There at last, a perfect figure,
heart for xylarium, soul to arboretum,
an ash queen shining
on her grove of gold.[33]

CELTIC TREE ZODIAC

HAZEL

5TH AUGUST–1ST SEPTEMBER

Otherworldly and irrepressible in equal measure, you possess a unique ability to regenerate. Always positive and energetic, you bend and pleach to support others, whatever their burden. Your generosity regularly involves nurturing those around you, plying them with a harvest of goodness, however tiny and precious. While everyone recognises your fierce intelligence, some believe you have magical powers to bewitch and enthral the supernatural. Compatible with Hawthorn and Rowan.

BRAMBLE

2ND SEPTEMBER–29TH SEPTEMBER

You may come across as indecisive but only because you like to explore every opportunity as you develop. While you may be resistant and capable, you do rely a lot on others to help you get along. Luckily for those around you, your generosity knows no bounds and you tend to form tight and fruitful bonds with your nearest and dearest. Compatible with Hazel and Willow.

SEP

OCTOBER

A good October and a good blast
to blow the hog acorns and mast.[34]

THE MONTH AHEAD

Now the days are shortening and growth is ceasing in our trees, life for those who care for trees is getting busy. The ancient Celts celebrated the arrival of autumn with the festival of Samhain.

Apples and pears are ready for harvest in the orchard, while in the forest, trees can be felled and preparations made for tree planting.

Wildlife is busy stocking up for winter, making the most of a bounty of fruits and nuts from our trees. Keep an eye out for the industrious jay in the park and forest, hiding acorns for feasting later in the winter but also sowing oaks in the process. Deer begin rutting and their awesome displays can be watched in locations right across Britain and Ireland, including in some of our town and country parks (e.g. Phoenix Park in central Dublin). Less dramatic, yet equally special, fungi of every colour and type imaginable erupt from trees, logs and the forest floor.

Children and adults alike can take up the challenge of nurturing a champion conker. If you are lucky to have access to an apple tree, don't allow any fruit windfalls to go to waste. Follow a delicious recipe for (spiced) apple chutney on page 252.

DATES OF NOTE

3 First day of Rosh Hashanah *(Jewish New Year)*
4 Feast of St Francis of Assisi
11–12 Yom Kippur
17 First day of Sukkot
25 Simchat Torah
27 Daylight saving time ends *(clocks go back)*
28 October bank holiday *(Samhain, ROI)*
31 Halloween *(All Hallows' Eve)*
31 First day of Diwali

OTHER SPECIAL EVENTS

UK FUNGUS DAY: a day celebrating the UK's fungi, held during the first week of October.

GROWN IN BRITAIN WEEK: a series of activities promoting home-grown timber during the third week of October.

APPLE DAY will be celebrated over the 26–27th with events throughout the UK.

NATIONAL MAMMAL WEEK: activities celebrating British mammals during the last week of October.

MOON WOOD FELLING: 24th October–1st November.

PRACTICAL NOTES

IN THE GARDEN

As growth slows in the garden, trees and shrubs will reward you with a show of autumn colours. As leaves drop, sweep little and often to avoid dealing with mountains of decaying leaves and stems. Leaf mould is a great soil conditioner and easy to make by placing tree leaves in a plastic bin bag with some holes pierced through it, and then stored for a couple of years somewhere out of sight. The leaves of some trees break down better than others, with alder, ash, birch, cherry, hornbeam and oak being among the fastest. Most conifer leaves (needles) will take as long as a couple of years, as will the thicker leaves from beech, sycamore, sweet chestnut and walnut trees. These can be shredded to speed up the process, while some like cherry laurel and holly will need to be shredded first. If you have acid-loving (ericaceous) plants in the garden, you could separate out conifer foliage to make a separate leaf mould, which is very beneficial as a top dressing for these plants.

Towards the end of the month, trees and shrubs are increasingly likely to be dormant, especially if there has already been a cold snap. This is a good time to move any plants and to plant new ones.

Any remaining late-cropping apples, together with pears, should be ready to harvest. If you have a lot of trees, then you may want to consider investing in a press to make your own juice. Apples can be stored, with some varieties even improving in taste. Treat every fruit with gentle care and do not attempt to store any with bruises or obvious damage. The best results come from wrapping every fruit in a sheet of newspaper and storing them in single layers in shallow cardboard boxes in a dark cool room. Check regularly for spoiling. Late season apples and pears can last up to three months.

If you have space in your freezer, cooking apple, pear or plum fruit is an easier way to store for later use. Peel, core and chop apples and pears before gently simmering in a pan for a few minutes until soft. Allow to cool before portioning into freezer bags.

In Britain, Apple Day is celebrated on 21st October or the nearest weekend, which this year falls on 26–27th October. If you want to identify any variety from your garden or orchard, take some along with you in case you come across an expert.

IN THE FOREST

The tree planting season starts next month, and if you are intending to plant you will already have planned by ordering trees. If you are planting more than half a hectare (which will require at least one thousand trees), you will have ordered perhaps one or two years previously, especially if you want local provenance (origin) material or more unusual species. Ground preparation might be necessary, for example to reduce soil compaction, improve drainage or control pernicious weeds. If you are planning to erect a fence to protect the young trees from rabbit, hare or deer, then now is the time to get this installed. Fencing is cheaper than having individual guards over a certain area of ground, so calculate the options carefully. Finally, if you are using tree guards, try to choose a plastic-free version. There are a growing number of options now available. Don't forget the sustainability of the tree stakes either. The market is dominated by treated softwood tree stakes but consider sourcing home-grown sweet chestnut stakes which are stronger and often last longer in the ground.

If you are felling trees for timber, note that the moon wood period this month is 24th October–1st November (see Tree Tides on page 81).

SUN AND MOON

SUNRISE AND SUNSET

DATE	SUNRISE	SUNSET
1 OCTOBER 2024, TUESDAY	7:20	18:55
2 OCTOBER 2024, WEDNESDAY	7:22	18:52
3 OCTOBER 2024, THURSDAY	7:23	18:50
4 OCTOBER 2024, FRIDAY	7:25	18:47
5 OCTOBER 2024, SATURDAY	7:27	18:45
6 OCTOBER 2024, SUNDAY	7:29	18:42
7 OCTOBER 2024, MONDAY	7:31	18:40
8 OCTOBER 2024, TUESDAY	7:33	18:38
9 OCTOBER 2024, WEDNESDAY	7:34	18:35
10 OCTOBER 2024, THURSDAY	7:36	18:33
11 OCTOBER 2024, FRIDAY	7:38	18:30
12 OCTOBER 2024, SATURDAY	7:40	18:28
13 OCTOBER 2024, SUNDAY	7:42	18:26
14 OCTOBER 2024, MONDAY	7:44	18:23
15 OCTOBER 2024, TUESDAY	7:46	18:21
16 OCTOBER 2024, WEDNESDAY	7:48	18:19
17 OCTOBER 2024, THURSDAY	7:49	18:16
18 OCTOBER 2024, FRIDAY	7:51	18:14

OCT

19 OCTOBER 2024, SATURDAY	7:53	18:12
20 OCTOBER 2024, SUNDAY	7:55	18:09
21 OCTOBER 2024, MONDAY	7:57	18:07
22 OCTOBER 2024, TUESDAY	7:59	18:05
23 OCTOBER 2024, WEDNESDAY	8:01	18:03
24 OCTOBER 2024, THURSDAY	8:03	18:01
25 OCTOBER 2024, FRIDAY	8:05	17:58
26 OCTOBER 2024, SATURDAY	8:07	17:56
27 OCTOBER 2024, SUNDAY (BST ENDS)	7:09	16:54
28 OCTOBER 2024, MONDAY	7:11	16:52
29 OCTOBER 2024, TUESDAY	7:13	16:50
30 OCTOBER 2024, WEDNESDAY	7:15	16:48
31 OCTOBER 2024, THURSDAY	7:16	16:46

* Sunrise and sunset times have been calculated for the centre of Britain and Ireland (a point just south of the Isle of Man).

OCTOBER'S MOON PHASES

2 OCTOBER	●	*New Moon*
10 OCTOBER	◑	*First Quarter*
17 OCTOBER	○	*Full Moon*
24 OCTOBER	◑	*Third Quarter*

NOTABLES

17TH The full moon is known as the harvest moon in Britain and Ireland. It is also a super full moon this month, appearing extra bright and large.

21ST-22ND The Orionids meteor shower, produced by dust grains left behind by the comet Halley, peaks overnight. Best seen after midnight as the Moon will be quite bright.

WILDLIFE

BIRDS

October is a time of plenty for birds feeding on nuts and berries. For the highly intelligent woodland specialist and member of the crow family, the jay, they overcome the glut of acorns (their favourite food) by stashing larders of collected nuts at multiple locations. Individual birds have been observed collecting and burying more than one hundred acorns a day, estimated to result in at least three thousand acorns stashed in a single autumn.

The birds return to their stash to feed throughout the winter, secure in having multiple larders just in case one is discovered by a mouse or rival jay. Inevitably, not every acorn is rediscovered, and so the jay becomes one of the most important methods of seed dispersal for oak trees. The collective noun for jays is a scold (see page 132 for more collective names).

INVERTEBRATES

Now that butterflies are less prominent, it is well worth looking for moths. Many are superbly camouflaged, so finding an adult in plain sight on the trunk of a tree, or a caterpillar mimicking a twig, is a great feeling. It is worth investing in a good field guide or perhaps a mobile app to help with identification when you do find one. Notable moths this month include the wonderfully named merveille du jour, which has spectacular cryptic camouflage of light green, black and white. It is almost invisible if resting on a tree because it looks like a dab of lichen. The adults can be seen feeding on late-flowering ivy in hedgerows, parks and woodlands.

MAMMALS

Our only prickly mammal, the hedgehog, will start its winter hibernation this month. It is one of only a few true hibernating mammals in the world, being more than simply asleep but capable of dropping its body temperature to match the surrounding environment and entering a state of torpor. Hedgehogs find a safe place in the bottom of a hedge (hence their name) or an old rabbit burrow for the winter, only emerging again in February. Each hedgehog has about six thousand spines and, underneath, a grey fur for insulation. Anyone who has picked one up, perhaps to rescue it from the side of a road, will discover it has surprisingly long legs! Hedgehogs are nocturnal mammals and have a mixed diet of earthworms, beetles and earwigs, but will also eat slugs, snails and dead animals. There are concerns for the conservation of the hedgehog which is thought to be in serious decline. This could be partly down to an increase in badger populations (the only mammals capable of unrolling a hedgehog), but more likely due to the increase in the road network and traffic.

October is the start of the deer rutting (breeding) season, which runs until mid-November. Stags (males) of our largest species, the red deer, operate harems of hinds (female red deer) which may number up to forty for the heaviest and fittest males. They protect their harems from all potential suitors. This will start with bellowing or roaring, the loudest and deepest signalling made by the larger stag. If roaring does not deter another stag, the two will walk in parallel, sizing each other up, before almost inevitably a head-on clash of antlers.

Another deer species, the naturalised fallow deer (first introduced by the Romans), behaves similarly to red deer, operating harems of does (female fallow deer). Our next smallest deer, the roe, behaves slightly differently, with up to four or five males controlling a group of hinds (female roe deer).

The sight of rutting deer is impressive, and fortunately happens right across Britain, including in London's Richmond and Bushy Parks, Exmoor National Park, the New Forest, Margam Park and Galloway Forest Park to name only a few. In Ireland, Killarney National Park is a great place to watch the spectacle.

PLANTS

If you are lucky to live near or able to visit some woodlands in the western parts of Britain or Ireland, it is well worth going in search of so-called 'lower plants' like mosses, lichens and liverworts. Many are quite difficult to identify, but one of the easiest is the leafy lichen known as tree lungwort. It grows in the precious temperate rainforests of Britain and Ireland (page 244).

FUNGI

October is the best month of the year to go for a fungus foray. Invest in a good guidebook or, if you prefer, an app for your phone, as there are many species to distinguish. Please remember that fungi can be deadly poisonous, and you are strongly advised not to taste any unless you are experienced in their identification, or even better, taking part in an organised event.

Fungi are considered one of the final frontiers in terms of ecology and scientific discovery. We are only beginning to understand the wonderful and mysterious lifecycle of fungi and their role in habitats, tree and soil ecology, and more. The mycelia (equivalent to a root network) run through the soil and interact with plants, even spreading up through the wood of living trees where they can coexist with them without causing any harm, until some trigger will cause them to become parasitic. So, the fruiting bodies seen in the autumn are only the reproductive stage of the lifecycle of fungi, which otherwise surround us invisibly for much of the year.

Some of the easiest fungi to identify appear this month. The common puffball is found in many woodlands. When fully mature, even the lightest touch can cause it to explode and release millions of spores, hence its nickname, the devil's snuffbox.

The bright red crimson cap of fly agaric is strongly associated with fairy toadstools and is unmissable anywhere it grows, particularly in birch and pine forests. Traditionally, fly agaric was hung indoors to ward off flies as it contains a mild insecticide. Beware when handling, as this is a poisonous species.

Another species which is quite easy to identify is the amethyst deceiver, whose beautiful purple colour really stands out among leaf litter under beech and oak trees. It is edible with a good nutty flavour, however, it is called the deceiver for good reason, as it can be easily confused with the deadly poisonous lilac fibrecap.

TRADITION AND FOLKLORE

The last day of October in the ancient Celtic calendar was celebrated as Samhain (in Irish it means November). The fire festival marked the end of the light-filled and prosperous growing half of the year, and the beginning of the dark or dead half. This was the night that the Celt's ancestors rose from the dead after nightfall, and pranks and tricks were played on unsuspecting victims, only to be blamed on fairies and mischievous spirits. It coincided with the arrival of winter migratory birds such as geese and woodcock (page 282), which often fly under the pale glow of the Moon, adding to the spectre of ghouls in the night. Samhain was adopted by early Christians as All Hallows' or All Hallowmas Eve, later morphing into Halloween.

ARTS AND CRAFTS

APPLE CHUTNEY RECIPE

Making chutney is easy, and the results are delicious! This apple chutney makes a wonderful addition to a cheese sandwich. You can choose to add some spices, which make it extra tasty and the perfect accompaniment to strong blue cheeses. With the simple addition of a ribbon and a handwritten label, the gift of a jar of homemade chutney sends more love at Christmas time than almost any other present.

MAKES 6 MEDIUM-SIZED JAM JARS

Ingredients
1kg apples (cooking or a mix of cooking and dessert apples), peeled, cored and roughly chopped
225g onions, roughly chopped
110g sultanas (or chopped dates if you prefer)
15g table salt
350g granulated sugar
450ml malt vinegar
optional spices: 1tsp each (but no more than 4tsps in total)

ground coriander, mixed spice and/or ground turmeric.
If you like a little heat, add some chilli seeds, ground
ginger and/or paprika

Materials and equipment: 6 sterilised jam jars and a preserving
pan (or a large saucepan)

Method
1. Add all the ingredients to the pan and bring to the boil,
   stirring occasionally to dissolve the sugar.
2. Reduce the heat and simmer gently for 90 minutes. Stir
   occasionally, paying special attention to the bottom of the
   pan to prevent burning.
3. The chutney mixture is ready when it has thickened enough
   that a hollow made by a spoon drawn through it takes a
   moment to fill again with the mixture.
4. Spoon the warm mixture into the jars and seal with lids.
5. Store in a cool and dark cupboard. Flavour improves over
   time and it is best to wait at least eight weeks before consuming.

CHAMPION CONKERS

Selecting and preparing conkers for battle is part art and part science. It is true that some conkers may be naturally better than others and there are many secrets that have been handed down between generations.

Conkers drop from horse chestnut trees during September and October. Resist the urge to select the largest and heaviest, as they are not always the strongest (and can be easier to hit than small ones!).

You will need to create a hole through the middle of the conker to thread through a shoelace or string. Traditionally, a skewer heated until it was red-hot was used to burn its way through. Most people today use a drill bit and electric power drill. Whatever technique you choose, be careful! Protect your eyes and hands, and children should be supervised.

The conker should be further prepared before stringing. This is where the real art or science comes into play. Artificially hardening a conker, such as by boiling in vinegar, coating in varnish or gently baking, is 'dishonourable' in the eyes of many. One of the best techniques involves patience and fore-sight; simply collect one year and store until the next playing season, by which time they will have naturally dried out and hardened up. Few players are so patient. If you have access to a pig(!), you could try another technique which involves feeding them to the animal and waiting for them to 'pass through', allowing its stomach juices to harden them. Just make sure you wash your hands after handling!

A range of materials can be used to string a conker. Kitchen or garden string is usually the most accessible. Leather laces lend a classy air and can be easy to thread thanks to their stiffness. Modern players use cord with some elasticity which helps with the swing. Generally, the best length is about 60cm, allowing for the string to be wrapped a few times around the fingers for extra grip.

As for playing the game – its traditions, rules and techniques – that's another whole subject.

TREE OF THE MONTH

PEAR

Oh to be a pear tree — any tree in blooms!
With kissing bees singing of the beginning of the world![35]

Pear fruit is familiar to everyone, although the tree may be easily confused with an apple. Compared to apple, the leaves of a pear are more leathery and darker green above, and hairless on the underside. Pear trees typically flower two weeks before apple. In winter, you may notice how the branches of a pear tree are more uniform and vigorous looking than those of an apple.

It is believed that the Romans brought the domesticated pear to Britain, while another widely naturalised relative, the wild pear, arrived about the same time. Only one pear species is native in Britain or Ireland and it is one of our rarest trees. The Plymouth pear, as its name suggests, grows in just a few locations in south-west England. It is an unremarkable species to look at, and when growing in a Devon hedge is likely to be completely overlooked unless it has fruit on its spindly branches.

In the garden or orchard, choose the warmest spot and best soils for a pear tree as they are choosier than apple, although they grow better in clay soils. Although some varieties of pear can grow up to 20m tall and live for hundreds of years, others are perfect for the small garden when trained as a cordon or even in containers. Varieties grown on a Pyrodwarf® or Quince C rootstock will grow to a maximum of about 180–240cm in height and look wonderful on a patio. Pears should be watered well when becoming established and at any age during a spell of drought. Pruning is highly beneficial in promoting good fruiting. Scientists are concerned that diseases on fruit trees, like pear, are likely to increase with climate change, particularly with warmer summers.

Most pear varieties are not self-fertile, in other words you need to plant two trees that can cross-fertilise each other. Among the few self-fertile varieties is the well-known Conference. There are some three thousand catalogued varieties of pear, satisfying a wide range of different growing conditions and culinary requirements, whether for dessert, cooking or juicing.

Harvesting of pear fruit occurs between August and October, with most varieties being ready in September. The fruit should be picked before fully ripe when firm and swollen. They are normally ready to eat a week or two later, although some varieties need longer to be enjoyed at their best.

Pear fruit was once an important source of vitamin C thanks to its excellent storage properties, meaning it could last all through the winter. One of the most celebrated products of pear is the alcoholic drink perry, the equivalent of cider made from apple. Freshly squeezed pear juice is allowed to ferment with the help of natural yeasts. As in cider making, there are specific varieties of pear, described as sharps, sweets, bittersharps and bittersweets, which are blended to produce the perfect perry. Compared to cider, perry is often lighter in colour and more subtle in flavour. Consumers should be wary of 'pear cider', which reveals that this is the product of blended pear juice and apple cider. Perry on the other hand is pure fermented pear juice, strongly alcoholic and fabulously delicious!

Like all fruitwoods, the colour and figure of pear is beautiful. It is particularly prized by woodturners, so even small diameter branches can be turned into delightful items.

Every landowner should be encouraged to plant wild pears in their hedgerows, where they will be admired by walkers and sustain hungry winter birds.

BRANCH PRUNING

There are many reasons why trees may need to be pruned. It is sometimes necessary to remove branches on trees that are unhealthy, dangerous or those that affect the form of a tree. Other types of pruning include 'formative' pruning which is carried out to improve the shape of trees, for example to remove forks in young forest trees, or to improve shape and encourage fruiting in orchard trees. More specialist types of pruning are the shearing of Christmas trees, and grafting techniques used to create trees for the orchard and garden.

WHY PRUNE?

Foresters aim to grow trees without branches on the lower parts of the tree stem as this improves the value of the tree for timber. Every branch on a tree creates a knot inside the tree stem, and while these can create attractive figures in the wood, they can sometimes weaken the timber or be difficult for furniture-makers and others to work with and create a satisfying finish. In the garden or street, branches may need to be removed for visual effect or to improve safety for people.

HOW TO PRUNE

Try to avoid cutting branches much larger than your thumb (the 'rule of thumb'). Much larger than this and the wound could take years to heal. It is much less effort and safer to remove branches when this size. Be aware that branches are typically much heavier than they look. If in doubt, seek specialist help.

How you remove branches is important. When a living branch is pruned, never leave behind a substantial stump of the branch as it could take years for the tree to occlude (grow round) the wound, making it vulnerable to further damage. Equally, don't cut so tight that the main stem is damaged; look for a ridge between branch and stem, and try to keep this undamaged. If pruning a branch that is already dead, you may see the tree attempting to occlude the wound, in which case cut away the deadwood leaving the living tissue or 'callus collar' undamaged.

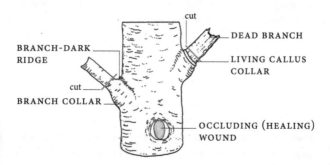

cut

DEAD BRANCH

BRANCH-DARK RIDGE

LIVING CALLUS COLLAR

cut

BRANCH COLLAR

OCCLUDING (HEALING) WOUND

PRUNING TOOLS

If complying with the rule of thumb (see previous point), secateurs, loppers and pruning saws are best. Make sure that blades are really sharp. Pruning saws are specialist tools, typically with their teeth set to work only on the pull stroke, making them very efficient to use. If you feel the need to resort to a bowsaw, let alone a chainsaw, you are probably attempting something at best too much for the tree, and at worst unsafe to yourself.

It is important to disinfect your tools when moving from tree to tree, so you don't spread any diseases. Use a strong concentration (at least 70 per cent) of isopropyl alcohol.

WHEN TO PRUNE

Most trees should be pruned when they are dormant during the winter months. For deciduous trees, this is when the leaves have fallen off. The exceptions in the forest are wild cherry and walnut trees. In the orchard, the same rules apply except for stone fruit trees, such as cherry and plum, as this can make them vulnerable to disease.

In the garden and orchard, some light pruning (i.e. formative pruning) of trained trees, such as cordons, espaliers, fans and pyramids should be undertaken in late August or early September.

CELTIC TREE ZODIAC

IVY

30TH SEPTEMBER–27TH OCTOBER

Your friendship bonds are legendary, and much admired by those outside your embrace. While it is true that you rely on others for much of your life, you particularly come into your own in later life. Your tenacity and determination to survive, even during the darkest of times, means that sometimes you can come into conflict with Bramble. Yet among friends, you are hospitable and reliable. Compatible with Ash and Oak.

REED

28TH OCTOBER–24TH NOVEMBER

Home is important to you, and wherever you are, you put down roots as deep as any tree. Whilst some may see you as hollow, you have a good heart. You protect and shelter those dear to you, like no other. You possess a creative spirit, in particular a talent for crafting words of beauty much admired by your friends. Being empathetic, you are often called upon by those in need, having the ability to soothe and nurture them while passing from one place to another, however other-worldly. Compatible with Ash and Oak.

NOVEMBER

Set trees at Allhallowtide and command them to prosper;
set them after Candlemas and entreat them to grow.[36]

THE MONTH AHEAD

If you go by the science or art (depending on your view) of moon wood felling, there are two periods which are best for harvesting trees this month. It's a time to trim and tidy in the orchard and garden, but don't be too zealous. Remember to share the remains of the autumn bounty with our fellow creatures.

The woodcock moon shines bright in the middle of the month. Keep an eye out for the arrival of these extraordinary woodland birds as they complete their 6,000km winter migration, piloted (as legend suggests) by our smallest bird, the goldcrest.

Now that leaves have fallen from most of our broadleaved trees, it could be a good time to learn to identify some of the conifers growing in our parks and forests. You never know, the skill may come in handy when you select your Christmas tree next month.

If you enjoy walking, there is nothing more satisfying than the companionship of a thumb-stick crafted by your own hand. Not only do they help while crossing rough ground, stiles or rivers, but their height and shape are perfect for leaning on while admiring the autumnal landscape, and for resting an elbow to steady binoculars while watching wildlife.

DATES OF NOTE

1 All Saints' Day *(and All Hallows' Day)*
2 All Souls' Day
5 Guy Fawkes Day
10 Remembrance Sunday
11 Martinmas
30 St Andrew's Day *(Scotland)*

OTHER SPECIAL EVENTS

NATIONAL TREE WEEK: a series of events in the UK during the last week of November.

MOON WOOD FELLING: ends 1st November; then 23rd November–1st December.

NOV

PRACTICAL NOTES

IN THE GARDEN

If you can find any holly with berries in the garden or in a nearby park, now is the time to pick some sprigs before the birds strip them off (but remember to leave some for them too). Until they are ready to bring indoors or to use for Christmas garlands, keep them outside in a bucket of water.

Any remaining tree leaves should be raked off your lawn and added to your leaf mould collection (page 240) or sent direct to a compost heap.

Evergreen hedges of box and yew should be pruned now. They will remain this shape now until new growth begins next spring.

IN THE FIELD AND ORCHARD

If you have any fruit in storage, picked during the last couple of months, keep an eye out for any that might be spoiling and remove them. You can start to give fruit trees their winter prune once all leaves have dropped. Out in the field or orchard, leave some windfalls where they lie for wildlife to eat over the winter months. They will be a major attraction for thrushes visiting Britain and Ireland from Scandinavia, namely redwings and fieldfares.

If you have any hedges, cut them or, better still, consider laying them (page 14). If you must cut any berry-rich trees or shrubs, pick some fruit-laden sprigs and hang them nearby for birds and small mammals to feed from.

IN THE FOREST

November and December are the best months of the year to plant trees. Extended periods of rain can create waterlogged conditions, whilst hard frosts can also occur, but provided that the ground is reasonably dry and frost-free, the fully dormant trees are most likely to survive the trauma of being transplanted.

Christmas tree growers will start harvesting trees this month, already fulfilling orders for corporate clients. Those dealing directly with the public often cut later or even to order in front of the customer (resulting in the freshest and longest-lasting cut tree).

If you are felling trees for timber, note that a moon wood period ends this month on 1st November, with another occurring 23rd until the end of the month (see Tree Tides page 81).

SUN AND MOON

SUNRISE AND SUNSET

DATE	SUNRISE	SUNSET
1 NOVEMBER 2024, FRIDAY	7:18	16:44
2 NOVEMBER 2024, SATURDAY	7:20	16:42
3 NOVEMBER 2024, SUNDAY	7:22	16:40
4 NOVEMBER 2024, MONDAY	7:24	16:38
5 NOVEMBER 2024, TUESDAY	7:26	16:36
6 NOVEMBER 2024, WEDNESDAY	7:28	16:34
7 NOVEMBER 2024, THURSDAY	7:30	16:32
8 NOVEMBER 2024, FRIDAY	7:32	16:30
9 NOVEMBER 2024, SATURDAY	7:34	16:29
10 NOVEMBER 2024, SUNDAY	7:36	16:27
11 NOVEMBER 2024, MONDAY	7:38	16:25
12 NOVEMBER 2024, TUESDAY	7:40	16:24
13 NOVEMBER 2024, WEDNESDAY	7:42	16:22
14 NOVEMBER 2024, THURSDAY	7:44	16:20
15 NOVEMBER 2024, FRIDAY	7:46	16:19
16 NOVEMBER 2024, SATURDAY	7:47	16:17
17 NOVEMBER 2024, SUNDAY	7:49	16:16
18 NOVEMBER 2024, MONDAY	7:51	16:14

19 NOVEMBER 2024, TUESDAY	7:53	16:13
20 NOVEMBER 2024, WEDNESDAY	7:55	16:12
21 NOVEMBER 2024, THURSDAY	7:57	16:10
22 NOVEMBER 2024, FRIDAY	7:58	16:09
23 NOVEMBER 2024, SATURDAY	8:00	16:08
24 NOVEMBER 2024, SUNDAY	8:02	16:07
25 NOVEMBER 2024, MONDAY	8:04	16:05
26 NOVEMBER 2024, TUESDAY	8:05	16:04
27 NOVEMBER 2024, WEDNESDAY	8:07	16:03
28 NOVEMBER 2024, THURSDAY	8:09	16:02
29 NOVEMBER 2024, FRIDAY	8:10	16:01
30 NOVEMBER 2024, SATURDAY	8:12	16:01

* Sunrise and sunset times have been calculated for the centre of Britain and Ireland (a point just south of the Isle of Man).

NOVEMBER'S MOON PHASES

1 NOVEMBER	●	*New Moon*
9 NOVEMBER	◐	*First Quarter*
15 NOVEMBER	○	*Full Moon*
23 NOVEMBER	◑	*Third Quarter*

NOTABLES

15TH The full moon is known as the woodcock moon (page 282). This is also the third super moon of the year, appearing extra-large and bright.

17TH The planet Uranus is at its closest approach to Earth. It will be visible all night long, appearing as a tiny blue-green dot.

WILDLIFE

BIRDS

Winter visitors like the woodcock (page 282) arrive this month. Redwings and fieldfares also arrive from Scandinavia, to miss the worst of an arctic winter and to feast on our hedgerows, particularly the haws of the hawthorn. Both thrush species are gregarious among their own kind, but very nervous, so can be difficult to approach. At first, they tend to be seen only in the open countryside, but as winter intensifies, they begin to visit parks and gardens.

The handsome waxwing also visits from Scandinavia and Russia, but only arriving in significant numbers when continental European winters are particularly harsh. Their plumage is reddish brown overall, including an attractive crest on the top of their heads, whilst their wings are barred gold and white, and they sport a black bib. They love haws and rowan berries.

INVERTEBRATES

One of our latest flying moths, the feathered thorn, may still be seen this month, or even in early December. The adult is well-camouflaged with red-brown wings, and feathered antennae, and can be seen in many parks and woodlands, but less commonly in urban areas. They lay their eggs on the stems of trees, often hidden among dormant buds where they are difficult to spot over the winter. Their larvae, which move by looping, look like twigs when still, and feed on a wide range of broadleaved trees.

PLANTS

Ivy is often in flower this month. It is a very important plant for woodland wildlife, providing food and shelter for countless invertebrates and birds. In the autumn, its small white flowers are an important source of nectar, especially when most other plants have finished flowering. Later still, its berries mature when many trees have been stripped bare, and are particularly loved by blackbirds, thrushes and pigeons. In the past, ivy has had a bad reputation among tree managers concerned about it restricting the growth of its host tree, or even making it more vulnerable to damage during winter gales, but there is little evidence of this in reality. Ivy is mildly poisonous if eaten and can cause a skin reaction for people who are sensitive to it.

Now that the leaves have fallen from deciduous trees, it is a good time to spruce up your conifer-identification skills. Can you tell the difference between a pine, cedar, fir and spruce?

FUNGI

Artist's bracket, a type of fungus which grows like a shelf bracket from an upright tree trunk, is easy to spot this month. It produces copious amounts of rust-coloured spores from its underside, which is made up of pores rather than gills. The spores stain the tree bark or any ivy leaves growing beneath. It is particularly common on old beech trees, where it feeds on the living wood as a parasite, breaking it down with special enzymes. The fungus can live for many years. Its pale underside is easily damaged or marked, meaning patterns can be drawn on it which never fade (hence its name).

If leaves fall not by Martinmas Day,
a cruel winter's on its way.[37]

TRADITION AND FOLKLORE

All Saints' or All Hallows' Day (1st November) was once another time for carolling, a tradition which is now limited to Christmas. Children would go 'souling' and hope for a soul cake (similar to a hot-cross bun but without the cross or the dried fruit) or a piece of fruit:

> *A soul, a soul, a soul cake,*
> *please God missus a soul cake.*
> *An apple, a pear, a plum or cherry,*
> *any good thing to make us merry.*[38]

Martinmas (11th November) was the traditional time for winter wheat to be sown, livestock to be slaughtered and for forest work to begin. Hiring fairs were held at this time for seasonal agricultural workers. It is now remembered as Armistice Day.

ARTS AND CRAFTS

There are few more satisfying things to make from the hedgerow or coppices than a thumb-stick. Walking sticks are designed to support the body's weight at waist height, and usually require some form of angled top which can be complicated to make (such as by steam-bending). On the other hand (excuse the pun), thumb-sticks are cut for the walker to rest their thumb in a simple groove and their length cut to rest comfortably at shoulder height (about 120cm). They are much better than a short stick for crossing rough ground and rivers, deterring overly inquisitive animals, determining the depth of boggy ground, and for leaning on while admiring a view. They are also the ideal height for resting an elbow while watching wildlife through a pair of binoculars.

A COUNTRY THUMB-STICK

The wood of most tree species will do, though ash or hazel are superior, being both lightweight and flexible. If you are prepared to deal with its vicious spines, blackthorn is a connoisseur's alternative. When determining the length of your stick, some people prefer a longer stick, which can be useful when descending steep hills or crossing water – generally, shoulder height or about 5cm below is ideal.

Materials and equipment: wood (as per the note above), a sharp pen knife (preferably with a lockable blade) and a pocket saw or secateurs

How to make

1. Look for a stem which is about 10–15mm in thickness and with a natural fork. It will need to have at least 120cm of straight stem below the fork. This is harder to find than you might think, so just persevere knowing that developing an eye for a good stick improves the more you look! When you are ready to cut, don't worry about perfecting the length; just make sure the stick is long enough, before you remove it using a saw or secateurs.
2. Once removed, cut off the two forked stems about 5cm above the fork.
3. Flip the stick upside-down so the forks are resting on the ground, and then estimate the perfect height for you. Mark the upside-down stick at this height, and then cut it to length.
4. Trim any side branches, whittle off any sharp stumps or knobs. At this point you have the bare bones of a functional thumb-stick. If you are already on a walk, you're good to go. If you would like greater comfort, an improved aesthetic and more durability, follow the remaining steps.
5. Improved looks will come from sanding any sharp or rough areas smooth, being careful not to remove too much bark as this provides natural protection to the wood. If the stick has any significant kinks, it can be straightened

by passing it over heat, traditionally it was held above the flames of a fire, though a heat gun is a good modern cheat. Once warm, flex it in the opposite direction to any bends or kinks by working it against your knee (wear thick trousers rather than shorts to prevent burning!).

6. Comfort for the thumb is much improved by widening and smoothing the thumb rest. A round dowel with fine sandpaper wrapped around it rubbed to and fro in the fork will eventually create the perfect cradle for your thumb, free of sharp edges and wide enough to avoid pinching.

7. Durability is increased by brushing on a light finishing coat of oil, such as Danish or linseed. It also gives the stick a lovely glossy look. Commercial stick ferrules can be purchased to prevent the stick's base from wearing. A good alternative is a short section of copper pipe salvaged from an old bathroom. Whittle the stick base as little as necessary so that the pipe almost fits on, then heat the pipe in a flame so it expands a little before slipping it on while hot. If done well it will never slip off.

8. Finally, enjoy using your thumb-stick and show it off to your friends at every opportunity.

TREE OF THE MONTH
NORWAY SPRUCE

Memories are lined by the smell of spruce[39]

Norway spruce is one of about thirty-three species of spruce which can be found growing around the world. As its name suggests, it is native to Norway and other parts of Scandinavia, where it grows across much of the country as far north as the Arctic Circle to the edge of the permafrost, and along much of its jagged coastline. Along with downy birch, which makes up much of the boreal forest, Norway spruce has a long history of traditional uses among the nomadic indigenous Sami people. The branches of the trees are often rich in arboreal lichens loved by reindeer, and single trees are often chopped down to feed passing herds. One of the oldest living trees is a Norway spruce growing in Sweden. Known as Old Tjikko, it is a clonal child of many generations of a tree growing for some 9,550 years!

Other notable spruces are the Serbian spruce, which dominates much of the rest of Europe, and Sitka spruce which is a species native to North America. Sitka spruce was introduced to Britain in 1831, primarily for its elegant pendulous branches when grown as a specimen tree in parks and gardens. It is an extremely hardy tree, growing in thin soil and severe environments in Alaska and as far south as California. It was these properties which ultimately made Sitka spruce one of the most useful trees for productive forestry on the uplands of Britain and Northern Ireland. Its uncreative use, planted in serried ranks up and down hills and mountains, led to it becoming synonymous with every aspect of afforestation in the first half of the twentieth century. The poor reputation of Sitka spruce is ill-deserved, as it is only its 'masters' who are to blame.

Norway spruce is one of the hardiest of trees, capable of growing almost anywhere, except where exposed to sea winds or urban pollution. Once it reaches about thirty years old, it produces some of the largest and most impressive cones, yet in Britain and Ireland it rarely produces viable seed, which is instead collected from tree nurseries in mainland Europe. The timber of Norway spruce is lightweight but strong. Its long fibres produce superior paper when turned into pulp. Slow-grown trees produce tonewood, prized by musical instrument-makers, and used, for instance, in the tops and sides of violins and cellos, and for guitar bodies.

To most people, Norway spruce is synonymous with the Christmas tree, even though other species that hold their needles better (e.g. European silver fir and Nordmann fir) are becoming more popular. Prince Albert popularised the Christmas tree, depicted when he and the royal family appeared in an edition of the *Illustrated London News* in 1848. Today, several hundred Christmas tree growers produce some eight million trees annually in Britain and six hundred thousand in Ireland for this lasting Victorian tradition. The Norwegian capital Oslo supplies London and Edinburgh with a Christmas tree, a tradition which started after World War II as a sign of gratitude to the Allies for their war aid. In a separate tradition, a Norway spruce is gifted at Christmas for the cathedral in Kirkwall, Orkney by the Fjære Historical Society, marking a connection between the countries which goes back to the twelfth century.

Christmas tree growers have to be attentive to tree quality, aiming to produce thick and bushy trees on a five–seven-year cycle. Trees are usually planted at 1 x 1m spacing, resulting in ten thousand trees cultivated per hectare (100 x 100m). Most growers produce under contracts with large firms, the trees being felled in November and sold to consumers via large retailers. Customers who want fresher trees, with needles less prone to dropping, should go direct to a tree grower and select their own tree from the barn, or even better, choose it when still growing in the field.

WOODCOCK MOON

The full moon in November is usually named the beaver moon in modern English, influenced by North American culture. Traditionally, in Britain it was known as the woodcock moon because it coincided with the arrival or 'fall' (see collective nouns on page 132) of the mysterious 'wader of the woods', the woodcock.

CREPUSCULAR

The European woodcock is a truly extraordinary bird, in appearance and behaviour. It looks like a snipe, but rather than frequenting mudflats like other waders, it lives in broadleaved woods. Its eyes are positioned high above its long bill allowing it 360-degree vision without needing to move its head. Its mottled brown plumage perfectly matches its woodland habitat of brown and russet winter leaves; a form of cryptic camouflage. It is active only at dusk and dawn, which is known as a crepuscular habit. Researchers have recently discovered that pale tips on its tail feathers are the brightest white of any bird in the world, and probably used to display to potential mates in the dim light while it's active.

FALL

Woodcocks are native to Britain and Ireland, and many birds choose to live in our woods and forests all year round. However, we also receive a massive influx or 'fall' of hundreds of thousands of birds every winter. Estimates by conservationists suggest that between 700,000 and 1,200,000 arrive during November, December and January. Each bird will have migrated 6,000km or more from the frozen steppes of northern Europe, the Baltic States, Russia and Siberia.

Although it is a threatened species due to loss of habitat, woodcock is still considered a gamebird in Britain. It is a prized quarry because of the difficulty of shooting one due to its camouflage and rapid zigzag flight when flushed.

WOODCOCK PILOT

Our smallest bird, the goldcrest, weighs about half as much as the familiar blue tit. Like the woodcock, large numbers arrive from Scandinavia in the autumn (although many of these tiny birds stay all year round). People used to think that they hitched a ride on the backs of woodcocks, hence their nickname the 'woodcock pilot'.

WOODCOCK MOON

A mere five thousand miles to fly;
rising from the Russian steppe,
and guided by a crest of gold,
to fall upon the English cold,
on the night of the woodcock moon.[40]

CELTIC TREE ZODIAC

REED

28TH OCTOBER–24TH NOVEMBER

Home is important to you, and wherever you are, you put down roots as deep as any tree. Whilst some may see you as hollow, you have a good heart. You protect and shelter those dear to you, like no other. You possess a creative spirit, in particular a talent for crafting words of beauty much admired by your friends. Being empathetic, you are often called upon by those in need, having the ability to soothe and nurture them while passing from one place to another, however otherworldly. Compatible with Ash and Oak.

ELDER

25TH NOVEMBER–23RD DECEMBER

Freedom-loving, wild at heart and fiercely independent, no one must stand in your way as you seek one challenge after another. Sometimes extrovert, blossoming with fruitful creativity, you also have a tendency to become withdrawn. Although you are generous and friendly, those who attempt to cut you down in any way will soon realise their folly. Compatible with Alder and Holly.

DECEMBER

If the sun shines through the apple tree on Christmas Day,
then apple trees will bear much fruit.[41]

THE MONTH AHEAD

Trees are fully dormant, so this month is a good time to prune them or take hardwood cuttings. This is the best month of the year for planting trees and creating hedgerows. Keep a look out for the extraordinary mistletoe, either to pick a sprig to liven up your love life or to watch for visiting thrushes gorging on their sticky berries. Holly berries, produced on female trees, reach their brightest crimson, perfect for adding cheer at Christmas.

This festive season you could try your hand at making your own Christmas decorations. Whether for your own home or as a gift, they are fun to craft.

There are two new moons this month, and the second one is always known as the black moon. Other heavenly interests include the murmuration of starlings as they prepare to roost. The awesome sight can be enjoyed almost anywhere in Britain or Ireland, especially above parkland in our towns and cities.

DATES OF NOTE

1 First Sunday of Advent
2 St Andrew's Day observed *(bank holiday, Scotland)*
8 Feast of the Immaculate Conception
21 Winter solstice
24 Christmas Eve
25 Christmas Day *(bank holiday)*
26 First day of Chanukah
26 Boxing Day *(St Stephen's Day)(bank holiday)*
31 New Year's Eve

OTHER SPECIAL EVENTS

29TH Festival of Winter Walks.

MOON WOOD FELLING: ends 1st December; then 22nd–30th December.

DEC

PRACTICAL NOTES

IN THE GARDEN

Collect evergreen cuttings from holly and other shrubs to make Christmas garlands and decorations. The cut stems of some bright-stemmed shrubs, like dogwood, also create eye-catching table displays and can be enhanced by adding battery-powered fairy lights.

Check tree stakes and ties holding up young trees before the worst winter gales come.

Hardwood cuttings can be taken from many trees and shrubs as an easy and reliable way of propagating them. The easiest are dogwood, honeysuckle, plane, poplar and willow. As long as it's not frosty, select and remove healthy shoots from the most recent year's growth. Cut off the tip and cut the remainder into several sections about 25cm in length, carefully placing each cut at an angle just above a bud. Dip the bottoms of each cutting in a hormone rooting powder and line them up in a trench dug in well-drained soil with plenty of good compost. Heel them firmly in, leaving about one-third above ground or enough for a couple of buds to emerge in the spring. The cuttings should have well-developed roots by the end of the next growing season (i.e. next autumn).

IN THE FIELD AND ORCHARD

Apples and pears should be pruned now, aiming to create well-structured trees without criss-crossing branches. This allows more air to circulate (which helps reduce the likelihood of some pests and diseases) and sunlight to reach the leaves.

Mistletoe will now be in fruit on apple trees and is often in reach. It is also found in poplar and aspen trees but is likely to be high up in the canopy. It is a hemiparasitic plant, meaning it generates its own resources through photosynthesis (like most plants) but benefits from additional resources by parasitising its host. If allowed to grow unchecked, it can weaken its host. If you want to grow your own mistletoe, find a sprig growing elsewhere and carry this to your host tree before attempting to pick off its very sticky berries. If you mimic the antics of desperate thrushes and fieldfares in trying to wipe the sticky residue off your fingers by smearing them on the branches of the host tree, you are likely to be successful in propagating it.

Now is a great time to plant a new hedge, with the trees and shrubs fully dormant. Place about four–five plants every metre, using a zigzag pattern rather than a single line as this creates a much denser hedge. Do include some standard trees (those that shouldn't be cut with the hedge), for example small species like field maple, rowan and whitebeam or occasional larger trees such as oak. Remember to take any browsing mammals into account by adding some sustainable protection for the young trees which will be vulnerable to damage.

This is the best month of the year to plant new trees in the orchard or park. Most people will purchase pot-grown trees and planting these larger trees successfully requires a few simple steps:

1. Remove the pot and gently remove any pot-bound roots that might spiral round. Trim away any broken or damaged roots. Soak the rootball in a bucket of water.
2. Dig the hole, making it twice the diameter of the rootball and a little bit deeper. Make sure the sides and bottom of the hole are not compacted (if so, loosen with a fork). Sprinkle some well-rotted compost or fertiliser in the bottom of the hole.
3. Place the tree gently in the hole. It should sit at the right depth so that it will be neither too deep, nor sit above soil level.
4. Back-fill with loose soil, mixed with compost and general-purpose fertiliser. This should be trodden down to compact it around the rootball.
5. Hammer in a tree stake at an angle facing into the prevailing wind direction (usually westward). The stake should cross the tree stem about 50cm above ground level. The general rule is to avoid too many stakes if possible, allowing the tree to create its own foundations.
6. Tie the tree to the stake using a suitable material. Rubber ties are effective but need to be loosened regularly. A natural material such as hessian can be very effective and naturally gives way over time.

Christmas tree growers will be in full flight selling trees to the public, though many will cut for business customers from November or even earlier. Trees are fully dormant this month, so now is a good time to plant new trees. Make sure you avoid planting if the ground is hard with frost as it can lead to root damage, or when the ground is saturated after heavy rain because it is difficult to make sure that the roots are well-covered or the soil overly compacted.

Coppicing can be undertaken, where hazel plants are cut at their base to stimulate regrowth on a regular cycle every five–eight years. If you want to propagate a hazel tree, you could try layering it. Bend a long stem down to the ground and peg or weight it down so it doesn't spring back up. Cover a section of it with a little soil where it touches the ground. By next summer the layered stem will have grown roots. If needed elsewhere, it can be cut free from its parent next winter and transplanted.

If you are felling trees for timber, note that a moon wood period this month ends 1st December, with another occurring 22nd–30th December (see Tree Tides page 81).

SUN AND MOON

SUNRISE AND SUNSET

DATE	SUNRISE	SUNSET
1 DECEMBER 2024, SUNDAY	8:13	16:00
2 DECEMBER 2024, MONDAY	8:15	15:59
3 DECEMBER 2024, TUESDAY	8:16	15:58
4 DECEMBER 2024, WEDNESDAY	8:18	15:58
5 DECEMBER 2024, THURSDAY	8:19	15:57
6 DECEMBER 2024, FRIDAY	8:20	15:57
7 DECEMBER 2024, SATURDAY	8:22	15:56
8 DECEMBER 2024, SUNDAY	8:23	15:56
9 DECEMBER 2024, MONDAY	8:24	15:56
10 DECEMBER 2024, TUESDAY	8:25	15:55
11 DECEMBER 2024, WEDNESDAY	8:26	15:55
12 DECEMBER 2024, THURSDAY	8:28	15:55
13 DECEMBER 2024, FRIDAY	8:29	15:55
14 DECEMBER 2024, SATURDAY	8:29	15:55
15 DECEMBER 2024, SUNDAY	8:30	15:55
16 DECEMBER 2024, MONDAY	8:31	15:55
17 DECEMBER 2024, TUESDAY	8:32	15:55
18 DECEMBER 2024, WEDNESDAY	8:33	15:55

19 DECEMBER 2024, THURSDAY	8:33	15:56
20 DECEMBER 2024, FRIDAY	8:34	15:56
21 DECEMBER 2024, SATURDAY	8:35	15:57
22 DECEMBER 2024, SUNDAY	8:35	15:57
23 DECEMBER 2024, MONDAY	8:36	15:58
24 DECEMBER 2024, TUESDAY	8:36	15:58
25 DECEMBER 2024, WEDNESDAY	8:36	15:59
26 DECEMBER 2024, THURSDAY	8:36	16:00
27 DECEMBER 2024, FRIDAY	8:37	16:01
28 DECEMBER 2024, SATURDAY	8:37	16:01
29 DECEMBER 2024, SUNDAY	8:37	16:02
30 DECEMBER 2024, MONDAY	8:37	16:03
31 DECEMBER 2024, TUESDAY	8:37	16:04

* Sunrise and sunset times have been calculated for the centre of Britain and Ireland (a point just south of the Isle of Man).

DECEMBER'S MOON PHASES

1 DECEMBER	●	*New Moon*
8 DECEMBER	◐	*First Quarter*
15 DECEMBER	○	*Full Moon*
22 DECEMBER	◑	*Third Quarter*
30 DECEMBER	●	*New Moon*

NOTABLES

7TH The giant planet Jupiter will be at its closest approach to Earth and therefore brighter than at any other time this year.

Use binoculars or a telescope to observe its cloud bands and some of its largest moons.

13–14TH The Geminids meteor shower is one of the best shows of the night sky. It can peak at 120 meteors per hour, many of which are multi-coloured. Coinciding with an almost full moon, only the brightest meteors may be visible this year.

15TH The full moon is known as the 'moon before yule' in Britain and Ireland, or the cold moon elsewhere.

21ST Winter solstice is the day when the day is shortest and marks the first day of winter.

30TH The second new moon in a calendar month is known as a black moon.

WILDLIFE

BIRDS

Rookeries always appear more prominent in the winter months, especially if you walk beneath one in a woodland when the birds will erupt in noisy 'caws'. December is also one of the best times of the year to watch starlings, which come together in huge numbers to roost in safety. The wheeling murmurations of starlings are one of the natural wonders of the world, especially when watched in front of a setting Sun.

One of our largest birds, the grey heron, starts to construct its nests in December as they lay their eggs in January. They nest in groups of up to forty pairs in the tops of trees, known as a heronry. The same nests can last for decades and might be used by many different pairs over the years.

The mistle thrush, which is larger than the more common song thrush, is one of the few birds which sings in December, especially from berry-laden trees which it defends from all comers.

INVERTEBRATES

Look for the winter moth, one of only a few moth species which fly in December. Females can't fly as they have short stubby wings, but the males have pale brown wings, which is perfect camouflage among winter leaves and tree trunks. In spring, the larvae are a staple diet for blue tits and great tits.

Early mornings laden with dew and mist are perfect conditions to spot spider webs. Usually, we may only notice a few prominent webs spun in silk among tree branches, but in the right conditions when the webs catch moisture in thousands of tiny pearl drops, it is astounding how many spiderwebs exist on every surface, from short grass and fences, to walls and tree branches, all of which we wouldn't normally notice.

PLANTS

Mistletoe is easy to spot in its leafless host trees this month. It produces white berries which are extremely sticky. Birds like the blackbird and aptly named mistle thrush have difficulty cleaning their bills when feeding on the berries. They resort to wiping them on tree bark and in branch crevices, and that's how the seeds are transferred to new host trees. There they begin to germinate, eventually forming a new bond with their host as their hypocotyl (type of root) burrows into the tree bark.

Among the often drab colours of winter, the red berries of holly and yew bring welcome cheer. The flesh of yew berries (technically known as an aril, a type of modified cone) is sweet, though the seed within, and every other part of a yew tree, is poisonous to mammals (but not to birds).

One of the few ground plants to flower this month is the white dead-nettle. Unlike its relative, the stinging nettle, the leaves and stems of white dead-nettle do not sting. It has pretty white flowers which provide a valuable source of nectar during hungry times for invertebrates. It grows in semi-shade along woodland rides and hedgebanks.

TRADITION AND FOLKLORE

Mistletoe (page 298) gained its name 'mistle' from the Old English for twig. Traditionally, mistletoe berries were seen as a symbol of male fertility, with the Ancient Greeks referring to them as 'oak sperm'. The plant gathered a mythical status among Ancient Britons, especially for druids. It was the Victorians who associated mistletoe with Christmas and the popular culture of kissing under it for good luck.

Traditionally, using holly without berries for decoration was considered unlucky, but was easily remedied by adding ivy with berries, in a custom known as holly boy and ivy girl.

ARTS AND CRAFTS

PINECONE TREES

These delightful eco-friendly Christmas decorations will attract lots of admirers in your home or office. Other conifer cones (such as spruce) can be used, though they don't work quite as well. Remember, it's not only the pinecones which originate from a tree, but the bottle corks will have been sustainably harvested from the inner bark of a cork oak (a relative of our native oaks, page 226), grown in Portugal or Spain.

Materials and equipment: pinecones (as many or few as you'd like!), old bottle corks, icing sugar, glues (water-based, plus a household glue or glue gun), small paintbrush, craft knife, ribbon and other decorations (optional)

How to make
1. Store your foraged pinecones in a plastic bag in the fridge, ideally wrapped in damp kitchen paper, until ready for the next step.
2. The cones will remain tightly closed when kept cold and moist. After removing from the fridge, quickly dry them

with kitchen paper, then paint their entire surface with a water-based glue.

3. Roll the tacky cones in icing sugar until covered all over. Stand upright to dry (an old egg carton is useful for this).

4. While the glue dries, make a base for each by cutting a cork in half with a craft knife. The top part of a large cork, such as a champagne cork, is particularly suitable (being a little wider and heavier than a standard wine cork).

5. Once the glue has dried, stick the cones to their cork bases using a thick household glue or, better still, a glue gun. Again, placing them in an old egg box helps stabilise the joint as the glue hardens.

6. You will now have a cone firmly stuck on top of a cork base which resembles a snow-covered tree. For a completely natural look, your work is complete. If you prefer a tree with decorations, you could wrap some brightly coloured ribbon around the cork base, and even make a miniature bow for the top of the tree.

7. As the tree warms up to room temperature it will open its scales, accentuating its snowy 'branch' tips. A collection of pinecone trees along the mantlepiece or windowsill looks very festive.

Alternative: for an even easier craft project, you can simply complete the steps 1–3 and hang the cones (i.e. without a base) from a Christmas tree as eco-friendly 'baubles'.

TWIG DECORATIONS

A range of different decorations can easily be made from twigs collected from a walk in the park or woodland. You could seek out particular trees with attractive twigs, like the bright bark of silver birch, or the red or yellow stems of different dogwood varieties.

Materials and equipment: tree twigs, secateurs and string, twine or coloured wool

How to make
1. Sketch out the design you like, to the scale you want (see the illustration below for ideas).
2. Trim the twigs to the lengths required.
3. Tie the twigs together with the string or wool of choice.
4. Hang from the Christmas tree, mantlepiece, or in front of windows.

TREE OF THE MONTH

HOLLY

Of all the trees that are in the wood, the holly bears the crown.[42]

Holly is widespread in Britain and Ireland, found almost everywhere except in a few areas of Scotland. Despite its association with winter and Christmas, the tree does not grow well in areas prone to prolonged frost, such as in cold hollows. It also does not thrive in waterlogged soils. It is relatively unusual among our native trees in being an evergreen broadleaved tree. Its dark, glossy leaves help it thrive under the shade of other trees, especially in oak and beech forests. Each leaf is retained for three or four years before dropping, making it highly efficient in growing in the understorey.

One of the most amazing properties of this small tree (which typically grows only up to 10m tall), is that it only has prickly leaves at its base. Higher than the first 2m above ground level, its leaves usually have smooth unprickly margins. The tree has evolved to 'understand' that it only needs to protect its highly palatable leaves from browsing mammals on those branches which are within reach. Even so, holly trees often show a 'browse line' where leaves have been stripped off by deer, domestic livestock or horses. Young trees are prone to browsing too, often limiting their ability to regenerate naturally.

Holly has separate male and female trees, so it's dioecious, rather than monoecious like most trees. This is why some trees have no berries, in other words these are male trees. Female trees don't flower until about twenty years old. They produce white flowers in early summer which are insect-pollinated. The best years for bright red crops of berries tend to follow a warm previous summer and a recent spring without any late spring frosts. As the berries remain on the tree during the winter, they are gradually softened by frosts and become increasingly palatable to small mammals and birds. Holly trees are not associated with many invertebrates, although the beautiful holly blue butterfly lays its eggs among the leaves for its larvae to feed on during the summer.

Seedlings can be propagated with patience. Each berry contains four seeds which can be grown with some patience. The seed is deeply dormant and needs at least forty weeks in a cool temperate (15°C) followed by another twenty-four weeks at 4°C (i.e. it requires more than one year of pre-treatment before sowing). Semi-hardwood cuttings taken with a heel can be collected in summer and planted out in pots in a shady position. If you have an existing tree in the garden or forest, it is easy to propagate by layering, which involves bending a living branch to the ground and covering it with a little soil where you want it to root.

The wood of holly is very pale and one of our densest native timbers. It can be used as 'strings' of pale wood for inlaying in highly decorative joinery and it is a beautiful wood for turning or carving, its tight grain capable of being fashioned into a range of products with intricate designs. Although it seems a terrible waste, holly wood makes excellent firewood, which burns well whether wet or dry.

Holly is mostly associated with Christmas, its familiar prickly leaves and bright red berries adorning imagery on cards, decorative garlands and even the top of the Christmas pudding. The association started with pagan druids, who believed that its evergreen properties meant it possessed sacred qualities capable of warding off evil spirits. Modern spiritualists believe that a sprig of holly will ensure good dreams and powerful visions when hung above the bed. Traditionally, holly was associated with fertility. Christian beliefs include the legend that Christ wore a crown of holly at his crucifixion, and its white berries forever took on the colour of his blood. This belief is central in the words of the traditional carol, 'The Holly and the Ivy'.

THE HOLLY AND THE IVY

The holly and the ivy,
when they are both full grown,
of all the trees that are in the wood,
the holly bears the crown.

O, the rising of the sun
and the running of the deer,
The playing of the merry organ,
sweet singing in the choir.[43]

HOW TO CHOOSE AND
PLANT A TREE

PLANT TYPES

When deciding to plant a tree there are a few options to consider, among them the size of tree. Your decision will not only
impact the cost of purchasing the tree, but also the effort of
planting and caring for it afterwards.

BARE-ROOT TREES

Bare-root trees are grown in large open beds in a tree nursery
and lifted so that their roots are free of soil. This means that
they are relatively cheap to produce, not bulky to transport,
nor heavy to lift. However, the technique only works for the
smallest trees (typically a maximum of 90cm). Their naked
roots are vulnerable to damage, particularly to drying out.
Bare-root trees are traditionally the choice of foresters when
planting many thousands of trees (with other options prohib-
itively expensive) and the workforce needs to be skilled. The
planting window for bare-root trees is limited to about two
months before Christmas across the south of Britain, and in
the north, and in Ireland until the end of March – however
climate change is affecting these times.

DEC

CELL-GROWN TREES

A compromise between bare-root and pot-grown, cell-grown trees are cultivated in small 'cells' or miniature plugs, and sold when young and small (typically 20–40cm tall). Often grown from seed in the same cell, they have well-formed roots in proportion with their stems which remain surrounded by soil. Their main advantage over bare-root trees is that their roots, especially fine feeder roots, are less exposed to damage by bad handling (especially drying out). This extends the season when they can be planted from October to March each year right across Britain and Ireland. They tend to be less affected by drought following planting and establish quickly. The disadvantage of their higher purchase price compared to bareroot trees is easily defended with improved rates of survival and early growth.

POT-GROWN TREES

Pot-grown trees are almost entirely limited to use in the orchard, park or garden. Exceptions might include certain native trees that dislike being transplanted, for example holly or yew. Their large size, and therefore high cost, means more investment in every sense. Each tree requires more effort to plant and to care for in the early years. Pot-grown trees often grow little in the first couple of years after planting as their roots become established and take time to grow in better proportion to their canopies. They require staking to prevent damage to the roots, and watering in their early years.

HOW TO PLANT A TREE

Regardless of plant type, there are many common tips and techniques for planting a tree. The best time of year to plant a tree is when it is dormant (November–March), and although pot-grown trees can be planted at other times they will require a great deal of care (page 292). Never plant a tree in a hole which is too shallow or too deep; look at the tree stem for the old soil level, and make sure that the soil in the new hole comes to the same level. Regardless of whether the tree is large or small, avoid including pockets of air around the tree roots.

Forest trees are usually planted quickly and efficiently, at a rate of perhaps one every minute. The small size of the cell-grown or bare-root trees enables dozens of them to be carried in a planting sack worn over the shoulder (keeping their roots away from sun and wind). A simple slot or a 'T'-shaped double slot is made in the soil and the tree carefully dropped into the hole before being firmly stamped down to remove air pockets. Trees this size do not need to be staked, although some form of mesh guard held up with a cane or small stake is often used to keep away browsing mammals (such as rabbit, hare or deer).

TREE SOWING

Of course, tree seeds can be sown to regenerate naturally although the results can be difficult to predict. Some trees require multiple periods of chilling to start to germinate, others with hard seed coats need scarification (abrasion). Planting seedlings or transplants is therefore less hit-and-miss. However, some trees are best grown from seed, one example being walnuts. Their taproots can grow up to one metre from the seed (the nut) before the shoot appears above ground. They also dislike having their taproots cut in the nursery or being restricted by containers. If you can find a fresh (green) walnut, simply bury it where you want it to grow in soil twice its diameter deep. Some farmers have experimented by creating new woodland by sowing tree seeds blended with wheat, the latter harvested after one year, leaving behind a field of young seedlings that take over in the second year, in a system called taungya.

CELTIC TREE ZODIAC

ELDER

25TH NOVEMBER–23RD DECEMBER

Freedom-loving, wild at heart, and fiercely independent, no one must stand in your way as you seek one challenge after another. Sometimes extrovert, blossoming with fruitful creativity, you also have a tendency to become withdrawn. Although you are generous and friendly, those who attempt to cut you down in any way will soon realise their folly. Compatible with Alder and Holly.

BIRCH

24TH DECEMBER–20TH JANUARY

You are a pioneer, quick to grow and prosper. Your presence provides grace and beauty but you have great strength and tolerance. Your caring nature means that others near you always benefit and you are not unknown to sacrifice yourself for others. You like to be among others of your kind. Even in death, you provide homes and food for others. Compatible with Bramble and Willow.

THE LAST SUPPER

Pick a planet.
Stir gently.
Do not overheat.
Share generously.[44]

GLOSSARY

Bark: the outer layer of the stems and branches of **trees**.

Broadleaved: **trees** that are usually **deciduous** with more or less wide leaves, cf. **needles**. Botanically known as angiosperms.

Budburst: the moment when the leaves inside a tree's bud are visible for the first time, often used by people studying **phenology**.

Canopy: the leafy area of a tree in its crown.

Catkin: the male reproductive structure or **flower** produced by some **broadleaves**.

Cone: the reproductive structure of a **conifer**, normally woody but it can be fleshy (e.g. juniper).

Conifer: trees that are usually **evergreen** with **needles**, usually bearing **cones**. Botanically known as gymnosperms.

Coppice: (*verb*) to cut the stem of a **tree** to stimulate growth of multiple stems from its base (known as a coppice stool); also (*noun*) an area of coppiced trees.

Cultivar: a variety of **tree** or other plant cultivated deliberately by breeding.

Deciduous: **trees** whose leaves die during the autumn, cf. **evergreen**.

Dormant: a period when trees rest during unfavourable conditions (e.g. the cold of winter).

Evergreen: **trees** that always retain some leaves all year round, cf. **deciduous**.

Felling: cutting down a **tree**.

Flower: the reproductive structure of a plant.

Flushing: the emergence of leaves of **flowers** in spring.

Forest: an area of extensive tree cover, used interchangeably with **woodland**. When spelt with a leading capital (i.e. Forest) this is a legal term from the thirteenth century meaning where Forest Law applied, often referring to areas for hunting where there was low tree cover.

Fruit: the swollen ovary of a **flower** containing **seeds**.

Native: a plant or animal established without any interference from humans. In Britain and Ireland this is defined as 8,200 years ago.

Needle: the leaf of a **conifer** tree.

Phenology: the study of the timing of natural events.

Pollen: the male gamete (comparable with sperm in mammals) produced by male **flowers**, consisting of a fine powder which can cause allergies for some people.

Pruning: the removal of branches and shoots from a tree to affect fruiting or timber production.

Seeds: the reproductive unit produced by plants.

Species: a group of individual plants or animals related closely enough to be capable of breeding together.

Tree: a long-lived woody plant with an elongated stem supporting multiple branches, which typically grows from 1m to 115m in height.

Wood: the non-living and innermost part of a **tree** stem or branch that provides mechanical strength to the tree. Also used as an alternative term for a **woodland**, especially as a placename.

Woodland: an area of extensive tree cover, used interchangeably with **forest**.

SOURCES

1 **Rise Up** from *Tall Trees Short Stories* Vol.20 by Gabriel Hemery. Wood Wide Works (2020).

2 **As the day lengthens** traditional proverb.

3 **When the woodpecker cries** traditional proverb.

4 **Here we come a-wassailing** traditional English song, variation on lyrics published in the *Bradford Observer* (24th December 1874).

5 **Wassail! Wassail!** from 'Gloucestershire Wassail', traditional song included in Dixon, *Ancient Poems Ballads & Songs* (1846).

6 **Shake and quiver** translated from 'Cinderella' in Grimms' *Fairy Tales* (1812)

7 **When the elm leaf is as big as a mouse's ear** traditional proverb.

8 **If Candlemas Day be fair and bright** traditional proverb.

9 **The snowdrop** traditional proverb.

10 **Make a fire of elder tree** traditional proverb.

11 **March winds and April showers** traditional proverb.

12 **When April laughed between her tears to see** from 'The Garden of Eros' in *Poems* by Oscar Wilde (1881).

13 **The alder trees** from 'The Battle of the Trees' in The Book of Taliesin VIII (c.1400).

14 **Ash before oak** traditional proverb.

15 **Thou wast not born for death** from 'Ode to a Nightingale' by John Keats (1819).

16 **In April I open my bill** traditional proverb.

17 **Ash new or ash old** from 'The Firewood Poem' by Celia Congreve first published in *The Times* (2nd March 1930).

18 **Beech wood fires burn bright and clear** from 'The Firewood Poem' by Celia Congreve first published in *The Times* (2nd March 1930).

19 **When the glow-worm lights her lamp** traditional proverb.

20 **White and odorous with blossom** from 'Trees' by Frank Stuart Flint from *Some Imagist Poets*. Riverside Press, Cambridge (1915).

21 **Beware the oak** traditional proverb.

22 **If Midsummer Day be ever so little rainy** traditional proverb.

23 **If it rains on Midsummer's day** traditional proverb.

24 **A swarm of bees in June** traditional proverb.

25 **St Swithin's Day if thou doest rain** traditional proverb.

26 **Til St James's Day is past and gone** traditional proverb.

27 **They planted me, a walnut-tree** a Greek fable presented as an epigram by Antipater of Thessalonica from *The Greek Anthology* Vol.3, trans. W. R. Paton, London (1917).

28 **August ripens** traditional proverb.

29 **Between every two pine trees there is a door** by John Muir (date of quote unknown), detailed in *Reinhabiting a Separate Country: A Bioregional Anthology of Northern California*, edited by Peter Berg, San Francisco, California: Planet Drum Foundation (1978).

30 **September blow soft** traditional proverb.

31 **This day they say, is nutting day** traditional proverb.

32 **If acorns abound in September** traditional proverb.

33 **All a spinney** from *Blough: An Anthology of Tree and Nature Poems* by Gabriel Hemery. Wood Wide Works (2022).

34 **A good October and a good blast** traditional proverb.

35 **Oh to be a pear tree** from *Their Eyes Were Watching God* by Zora Neale Hurston. University of Illinois Press (1937).

36 **Set trees at Allhallowtide** traditional proverb.

37 **If leaves fall not by Martinmas Day** traditional proverb.

38 **A soul, a soul, a soul cake** traditional begging song, transcribed by Rev. M. P. Holme in Lucy E. Broadwood, *English County Songs* (1893).

39 **Memories are lined by the smell of spruce** traditional quote (Anon.).

40 **Woodcock Moon** from *Blough: An Anthology of Tree and Nature Poems* by Gabriel Hemery. Wood Wide Works (2022).

41 **If the sun shines through the apple tree on Christmas Day** traditional proverb.

42 **Of all the trees that are in the wood** extract from 'The Holly and The Ivy' by Cecil James Sharp, *English Folk-Carols* (1911).

43 **The Holly and the Ivy** carol by Cecil James Sharp, *English Folk-Carols* (1911).

44 **The Last Supper** from *Blough: An Anthology of Tree and Nature Poems* by Gabriel Hemery. Wood Wide Works (2022).

FURTHER READING

Roger Deakin, *Wildwood: A Journey Through Trees* (Penguin Books, 2007)

Peter Fiennes, *Oak and Ash and Thorn: The Ancient Woods and New Forests of Britain* (Oneworld Publications, 2017)

Gabriel Hemery, *Blough: An Anthology of Tree and Nature Poems* (Wood Wide Works, 2022)

Gabriel Hemery and Sarah Simblet, *The New Sylva: A Discourse of Forest and Orchard Trees for the Twenty-First Century* (Bloomsbury Publishing, 2001)

Fiona Stafford, *The Long, Long Life of Trees* (Yale University Press, 2017)

Colin Tudge, *The Secret Life of Trees: How They Live and Why They Matter* (Penguin Books, 2005)

Peter Wohlleben, *The Hidden Life of Trees: What They Feel, How They Communicate* (William Collins, 2017)

ACKNOWLEDGEMENTS

I am forever indebted to Guy Whiteley, whose celestial powers aligned the principal bodies of this project.

I am very grateful to Emma Smith and the tremendous team at Robinson/Little, Brown for their passion and dedication, namely Amanda Keats, Bekki Guyatt, Gemma Shelley, John Fairweather and Linda Silverman. A heartfelt thanks to Charlotte Day for bringing life to my thoughts and ideas through her wonderful illustrations.

Finally, to my wife, Jane, for her unerring support and to my whole family for their tolerance of my writing habits.

ILLUSTRATIONS

All full-page chapter openers by Charlotte Day, along with illustrations on pages 23, 28, 35, 48, 50, 72, 74, 97, 98, 122, 127, 147, 156, 170, 195, 197, 221, 222, 246, 247, 272, 284, 297 and 299.

Illustrations on pages 14, 201, 260 and 303 by the author.

Images on pages 55 and 59 by Clare Sivell.

All other illustrations by Shutterstock.

INDEX

326